What Industry Leaders Have to Say About
Don't Toss My Memories in the Trash

A book that guarantees a happy ending! With a heart for seniors and wisdom that can only come from experience, Vickie will expertly guide you down the road to a successful move.

Donna Smallin
Author, *The One-Minute Organizer Plain & Simple*

One of the most stressful times in life is during a move. Vickie has written the prescription to eliminate that stress through real life stories and easy to implement tips and ideas. With *Don't Toss My Memories in the Trash*, senior downsizing is no longer the tough decision it once was. If you are planning a move or senior downsizing, this book is a must!

Patty Kreamer
Author, *...But I Might Need It Someday!*
and *The Power of Simplicity*

What Industry Leaders Have to Say About
Don't Toss My Memories in the Trash

An invaluable, comprehensive and practical guide to help you or your loved ones transition easily to a new chapter in their lives. Vickie's compassionate approach and insight into the moving and downsizing process gives you the necessary tools to ensure a smooth and satisfying move experience.

Barry J. Izsak
President, *National Association of Professional Organizers*

If your or your parents are planning a move into a smaller home, this book will help you understand that it's not just about "stuff," it's also about the memories, emotions, and life stages that "stuff" represents. Vickie explores and explains the emotional terrain as well as the attic, basement, and china closet.

Peg Guild
President, *National Association of Senior Move Managers*

Don't Toss My Memories in the Trash

A Step-by-Step Guide to Helping Seniors Downsize, Organize, and Move

Vickie Dellaquila

Published by Mountain Publishing

Book Cover Design by Donna Herrle of Drawing Conclusions

Edited by Jennifer McGuiggan of The Word Cellar

Library of Congress Control Number: 2006908085

ISBN: 0-9788189-3-8
978-0-9788189-3-7

Printed in the United States of America

Requests for permission to make copies of any part of this book can be made by contacting:

Organization Rules, Inc.
412-913-0554
vickie@OrganizationRules.com
www.OrganizationRules.com

10 9 8 7 6 5

Acknowledgements

A warm thank you to:

Alison Conte for her involvement with this book. She shared her experiences and went through the process with her own parents, who recently downsized from their home of several decades.

Donna Herrle of Drawing Conclusions for the great book cover.

Jennifer McGuiggan of The Word Cellar for editing this book.

Peg Guild, Barry Izsak Patty Kreamer, Margit Novak, and Donna Smallin, for their kind words and input for this book.

Jody Adams, Patty Kreamer, Susan Lieber, Leslie McKee, Jill Revitsky, Nancy Scott, Ann Tomer, and all of the NAPO Pittsburgh organizers for their support and guidance.

Erin Claypool, David O'Brien, and Patrick Randall of the North Hills Senior Resource group for all of their help and support for my project.

All my dear, wonderful clients whom I have had the privilege of helping on the road to downsizing, organizing, and relocating.

*To my husband Phil
and my daughters
Angela, Katie, and Emily
for their continued
support and love.*

Tale of Contents

Introduction

Every year, thousands of seniors leave their homes.

Some no longer want the burdens of home ownership. For others, caring for a house has become too difficult. To ensure their safety, comfort, and happiness, they must leave their home of 20, 30, or even 50 years.

Relocation can be traumatic for all of us, and is certainly more so for older adults. The upheaval often starts by sorting through and disposing of furniture, clothing, and even precious possessions before moving into a smaller home.

This process is hard on older adults and on their adult children and others who assist in the downsizing process. Familial bonds can be stretched out of shape and close relationships may be tested. Children who live far away might suffer from guilt, and those who live close could be asked to deal with too much.

But, amidst the boxes, fading photos, and crumbling newspaper articles is an opportunity to grow closer to an older adult to make them comfortable and safe in a new home. And for the older adult who is moving, there is an opportunity to start a more secure and socially active way of life. The end of independent living should not be feared as the end of living.

This book will show you how to downsize, move, and live in a newly organized way, whether you are helping to relocate a parent, a friend, or even yourself. I address different groups of people throughout the book. Much advice is specifically meant for adult children and other family members who are helping a senior relative downsize and move. However, some of the book is aimed at the person who is moving, which in this case, is probably an older adult. But remember, most of this advice is applicable to people of any age who are relocating or simply seeking a more organized life.

Part One of this book considers whether and when to move to a smaller place. It reviews various arguments for relocating, which may be helpful if you or loved ones are still trying to decide. If that decision has been made, you can concentrate on Parts Two and Three, which relate to the downsizing process and moving into a new home.

I hope that you and *some* of your belongings are very happy in your new home.

Throughout this book, I refer to professionals who specialize in one or more fields. There are several national professional organizations that they may belong to, including the National Association of Senior Move Managers (NASMM) and the National Association of Professional Organizers (NAPO). Members of NASMM are known as Senior Move Managers, and members of NAPO are known as Professional Organizers. Because this book covers a wide area of service providers, including both Senior Move Managers and Professional Organizers, I refer to them simply as "professionals" throughout the book.

Note: The stories in this book are true, but the names of people have been changed to protect their privacy.

Part One – Is It Time to Move? Deciding to Relocate

"Things do not change; we change."

-Henry David Thoreau

Chapter 1: "I'm Not Going Anywhere"

Martha and Joe have lived in their three-story home for 46 years, raising two daughters, four dogs, two turtles, and a few goldfish. They once chased the girls up two sets of stairs. Now that they're older, it is a struggle to get up and down those steps.

Their daughters Cindy and Sheila have lives of their own and both live far away. But they are concerned about their parents' safety and their ability to keep up with their cumbersome old home.

These days, Martha does not always have the strength to carry items up the stairs, so she leaves things on the steps. This narrows the path and makes a difficult climb even harder.

Joe used to mow the lawn in no time. Now that expanse of green seems much larger and takes longer to tame. Cindy and Sheila have offered to pay for a landscaping service, but Joe really enjoys gardening and doesn't want to surrender his kingdom.

Martha was equally proud of her housekeeping, but she can't keep up with it anymore. Dust piles up on dressers; unused things accumulate into piles of clutter.

As they age, Martha and Joe find they are less involved in the clubs and activities that used to occupy them. While Joe still drives, Martha is not as comfortable behind the wheel. This restricts their social life.

For 10 years, Sheila and Cindy have tried to get their parents to think about downsizing and moving to an apartment or retirement community. Their arguments of "You could fall, and no one would find you," and "You'd be less isolated," haven't persuaded their folks.

Martha and Joe are not ready to give up their home with its wonderful memories. And while Sheila and Cindy, like other adult children, worry about their parents' safety, socialization, home maintenance, and general well-being, the decision to move must belong to the parents.

It can happen at age 60 or not until age 92. But at some point many older adults leave their long-loved family home and relocate to a smaller place.

Many couples are happy to move into a retirement community or a condo at the age of 65 or 70. They give up the lawn care, large heating bills, and some of the chores of their large, empty-nest house. They trade creaky pipes and a crumbling roof for a shiny new compact apartment – with plenty of room for the two of them and a second bedroom for visiting grandchildren.

But more often, there is extensive debate, if not actual distaste, for the idea of moving.

For many people, giving up the family home seems like losing a loved one. If the family is gone, the house is all that's left, containing the couch they snuggled on, the table where they ate, and the corner where the baby's crib sat. Though only memories linger, they can't give up such a physical connection to those rich and happy days.

In addition, many seniors perceive this loss of independent living as the beginning of the end. Some people think that if they move to an "old age home," they will face a dreary future of hospital-style rooms, illness, and death.

Still, seniors of 80 and 90 should not have to spend their days trudging up stairs, trying to carry laundry from the basement, and worrying that the next step will mean a fall and a broken hip. Shoveling walks, fearing crime, and living in isolation is no way to spend one's "golden years."

Fortunately, today's seniors have many options for easy-living, ranging from a comfortable cottage to a resort-style high-rise apartment. Even a "mother-in-law apartment" in an adult child's suburban home can be a safer, less taxing alternative.

Changes Require Changes
When Sheila and Cindy mention downsizing and moving to a more senior-friendly environment, their parents say: "We'll do it someday. We have lots of time."

Then Joe missed his footing coming down the stairs. He fell down the last three steps. Martha was able to get him up and into an ambulance. Luckily, no bones were broken. Joe spent a few days in the hospital. When he got home, they told Cindy that they were ready to relocate.

"I think it is our time to move," Joe says. "The fall scared me. This house is too big and unmanageable for us now. We need to downsize and move to a smaller home." Martha agreed reluctantly, but Sheila and Cindy are much relieved.

Like it or not, major changes in older adults' lives may prompt them to seek a new home.

Often, the decision to relocate comes voluntarily after a spouse's death or major illness. Since most older couples have traditional ways of dividing up household chores, it is difficult for one of them to assume all responsibility if the other is gone or cannot do his or her share. A man may feel helpless in the kitchen or laundry room without his wife. By relocating to a new apartment or community, he may be grateful for the extra help with these chores.

On the other hand, a widow may also feel lost in a big house – and unfamiliar with the ways of the furnace or the hot water heater. But in her new community, someone else takes care of general maintenance and mows the lawn.

When a single woman loses a long-time housemate, she may have no one left to talk to. The idea of cooking for one is disheartening, and the fun of commenting on silly television shows is gone. But after moving to a retirement community, she takes up new hobbies, watches weekly movies, and makes new friends.

If older adults wait too long, they may find that the decision is made for them. A broken hip often lands a senior in the hospital, then a rehabilitation center, and eventually, a long-term care facility as they recover.

To avoid this, it is important that children and neighbors monitor seniors' ability to care for themselves. As I will describe in later chapters, some safety hazards become more of a problem when adults grow unsteady on their feet, become frail, or develop vision problems.

Chapter 2: Make the Choice While You Still Can

At age 88, Gertrude had lived in her house for 51 years. It has been three years since her husband died and her children have been after her to move to a smaller home. Gertrude was open to the idea and visited several retirement communities. She even put down a deposit on an apartment. But after thinking about it some more, she decided she'd rather stay in her home, and no one could change her mind.

Early one morning her son Randy received a call from Gertrude's neighbor. Gertrude had fallen the night before and lay on the floor for hours, unable to get up or call for help. The family's biggest worry had come true.

Gertrude's broken hip will heal, but her doctors have insisted that she not live alone after her recovery. Gertrude ended up moving to the retirement community where she had made a reservation. She did not want to move, but now she had no choice.

Her children had to go through the house and pack up her belongings. At first, it seemed overwhelming. After awhile, everyone was tired and just wanted to "throw it all in the trash." They just could not take any more time to deal with a massive, decades-long accumulation of stuff.

Gertrude enjoys the retirement community. She has made several friends and knows that help is available with just the push of a button. Still, it was difficult to adjust. Because she didn't make the move when she was healthy, Gertrude has regrets. She missed an important part of the transition: saying goodbye to her home and choosing what to let go of and what to keep.

Is it safe to stay in the old family home? Consider the house and your own mental and physical limitations as they impact your health and safety.

House Location and Construction

- Does the house have many narrow staircases? Do you have to use them to reach the bedroom, bathroom, or washing machine?
- Is the kitchen easy to get around in? Does reaching the sink, stove, or cupboards pose safety hazards?
- Are you able to keep up with home maintenance, or are things falling into disrepair?
- Is the house far from the supermarket and bank? Are sidewalks in good repair or are they crumbling and apt to cause a fall?
- Has the neighborhood changed? Is it safe to sit on the porch at night?

Physical Limitations

- Can you keep up with the housecleaning? Not being able to bend down to clean up spills can create a slipping hazard.
- Is your spouse's memory still good? Would he ever leave a pot boiling on the stove or turn on a burner and walk away? Could she leave water running in the tub until it overflows?
- Can you and your spouse handle your basic hygiene needs? Can you maneuver in and out of the tub or shower? Can you keep up with laundry, or do you need to send it out?

- Are you susceptible to home invasions and scam artists who prey on seniors by phone and in-person?
- Can you still manage to pay your bills?
- Are you isolated in your home? Is the letter carrier the only person you see all week?
- Can you continue to make healthful, appetizing, and nutritious meals? Or is food spoiling in the refrigerator?
- Do you take your pills on time and practice other needed medical care, like diabetes testing?
- Has driving become difficult due to your age?

Living alone can be risky for anyone, particularly for a senior. If the house is cleaned infrequently, dust and mold can accumulate and cause breathing difficulties. Fragile seniors are more likely to trip and fall over items piled on steps and as they negotiate walkways narrowed by boxes, piles of old clothes, and newspapers. When they are alone and isolated, they may be susceptible to depression and anxiety, not to mention con artists and thieves.

More Gains than Losses
Recently, a retirement community hosted an open house and luncheon for prospects. Various residents stood at the podium and expressed their opinions about living in their new homes. Many spoke about enjoying their new freedom from home maintenance, finding new friends and hobbies, and having help when they needed it.

David, a retired attorney, spoke about these things, but added something else. "Please think about downsizing and moving now. You think you have all the time in the world to take care of things later. Maybe you do, but maybe not. Do this when you are young enough to enjoy your new found time and friends. Do it while your mind and body are functioning well, because you never know."

He asked the older people in the audience, "Do you really want your children deciding where you will live, what will happen to your belongings, your home, your money, and your memories?"

David knew that it is more satisfying and more empowering to make your own decisions instead of letting your children do it for you. He also knew that it is no gift to leave your children with the tremendous job of going through your home and belongings.

Sadly, David passed away a few months after that luncheon. He was happy during his last few years, having made the decision to downsize and move while he was able to enjoy the benefits. David's children appreciated that their father had downsized and made his own decisions about what would happen to his home and belongings. It allowed them to enjoy time with their dad, rather than worrying about what needed to be done.

A move to a smaller, modern apartment or to a retirement community can have many benefits.

- Staff members regularly check on the health and security of residents.
- Housing is private, clean, and well lit. Rooms may be smaller, but are on one level, so residents can maneuver and even clean more easily.
- When meals are provided, seniors can eat more nutritiously without fussing with shopping, cooking,

and washing dishes. Meals are a chance to socialize
and create new relationships.

- Doctors, podiatrists, dentists, and even beauticians are
  available within the community. When seeing a doctor
  is more convenient, seniors stay healthier.
- Movie nights, college lectures, crafts, and computer
  classes offer a variety of new activities. Materials and
  instructors are provided, making it easy to pick up a
  new hobby or rejuvenate an old one. Suddenly, life is
  interesting again.
- Older adults have opportunities to swim, exercise, and
  learn tai-chi, which engage the mind and the body,
  staving off illness, obesity, and keeping them mentally
  fit.

Maybe the idea of downsizing and moving makes you feel
anxious. But think about how much you'll gain, especially
when you choose your new home for yourself!

Chapter 3: Persuading Loved Ones to Move

Harold had a long, wonderful career as a top salesman for a well known company. He loved his career and the luxury of traveling all over the world. But he also loved to come home to his small, well-kept home. Never married, Harold had no children and just a few long-distance relatives.

After his retirement, Harold was free to pursue his many interests and hobbies. He was having a great time writing, doing research for organizations, and going to the symphony. But then he had a stroke at the age of 81. During his rehabilitation, he stayed – none too happily – in an assisted living home. He worked hard to regain much of his strength.

Luckily, before the stroke, Harold had given his friend and financial advisor, Gary, Power of Attorney. Gary helped Harold through the stroke and watched his progress during recovery. He noticed that Harold was not the same after the stroke. His memory started to fail, his balance was off, and he needed assistance to do many daily tasks.

However, Harold didn't see this deterioration and had made up his mind to go home. When Gary hired me as a professional organizer, he hoped I'd help make Harold's little home safer for him to live in after he left the assisted living community.

I met Harold at his home. He had accumulated many papers throughout his career and he enjoyed going through them with me. But he tired easily and relied more and more on my help. As time went on, Harold grew weaker, and began to use a cane.

*One day, Harold told me, "I don't think I am going to be able
to come back and live in my home. I really want to, but I now
realize that it is not going to happen." It took some time – and
actually being in his home – for Harold to come to the
conclusion that he was no longer able to live alone. Even
though it is not the outcome he would have liked, he was
happy that he was able to make the decision himself.*

If you feel that a loved one is unsafe at home, you may need to
work hard to convince him or her to move. Often, the
arguments for relocating seem clear to everyone except the
senior who needs to make the change.

One strategy that can work is to casually introduce the idea,
and just leave it at that. Like a cup of tea, sometimes an idea
needs to brew on its own to come to full flavor. Try
mentioning someone you know who now enjoys living in a
local retirement community or new condo. While folding the
laundry or doing dishes, comment on how nice it would be to
have weekly maid service. Give the person a few weeks to get
used to the idea before bringing it up again.

You may find that there is less resistance than you thought.
One man thought he would have a hard time convincing his
elderly aunt to leave her city apartment of 50 years and move
to a quiet suburb. It turned out that she was more than ready to
go. Her city neighborhood had changed drastically over the
years, and now she was afraid to even walk around the block.

On the other hand, your relative may be uninterested, or even
insulted, by the idea. So introduce it gradually, and give the
idea some time to simmer.

Financial Problems

Some seniors assume they will not be able to afford the high upfront or monthly costs of a retirement community. They may already be uncomfortable with living on their savings without generating a weekly salary.

By researching the actual costs of independent living or long-term care communities, you will have some solid financial data to use in your decision making. There are many options for retirement living, and while some do have entrance fees, others just expect a typical monthly rent.

However, some older adults have unrealistic perceptions about the expenses of paying for a home in a retirement community. Point out that they can cut back on some of the expenses they have now – or may have in the future if they stay in their aging home. These costs may include gas, water, sewage and electricity bills, and hired help to clean, do laundry, or mow the grass. Are the furnace and the plumbing system aging? Is the roof or water heater due for replacement? Those things add additional expenses.

Health related costs should also be considered. If Mom or Dad continue to live on their own, will they eventually need a home health aide to help with daily living activities? In a long-term care community, these services are often included. Having a doctor or nurse on the premises may eliminate the need for expensive taxicab rides, homecare nurses, or pharmacy deliveries.

A Matter of Perception

Bill, a well known local artist, moved from Florida to New Jersey to be near his daughter, Donna. "Dad, you are 84 years old and I am worried about you," she said. "I'd love it if

*you were closer." Bill loved his Florida neighborhood, but
reluctantly agreed to move into an apartment in a New Jersey
retirement community.*

*As the packed boxes piled up in his new apartment, Bill felt
he'd made the wrong decision. As he unpacked his paintings
and art supplies, he became depressed, missing his artistic
friends down South. He didn't even have room to hang his
work in his new home.*

*Then the directors of the retirement community approached
him about teaching a painting class. Bill thought about it and
agreed to give it a try. Not only did he find that he loved
teaching others about painting, but his paintings found a new
home, exhibited in one of the common buildings. Residents
enjoyed seeing them and meeting the local artist. Bill
continued to teach and has since connected with other local
art groups who have displayed his work.*

*When people change locations and give up the demands of
homeownership, many of them discover new communities, new
relationships, and new ways to put their talents and skills to
work.*

If your parents are reluctantly clinging to the home and life
they have known for decades, try to help them see how they
are changing as individuals. Start a conversation about how
they once made the transition from college student to
breadwinner.

Ask your aging parents how they see themselves now, saying
"Is your home dedicated to a former life? Don't you deserve
more?"

You may also need to change their mental image of an "old folks' home." Take your parents to a retirement community open house or tour so they can get a feel for the services and activities that are offered.

This shouldn't be a pitch, just a visit. If a tour isn't available, visit a friend or relative in a retirement community. Try to keep the discussion general, and avoid any mention of relocating. When your parents return to their aging home, it may get their wheels turning. But do start the discussion early enough so that the senior has several months to consider the idea and select an option that he or she is comfortable with. Many communities and apartment complexes have waiting lists of several years, so there will be plenty of time to get used to the idea, make plans, and carry out the downsizing and relocation.

Chapter 4: Housing Options for Seniors

At retirement, many adults are still young-at-heart, healthy, and active. Throughout their 60s, 70s, 80s, and beyond, they still enjoy gardening, golf, and tennis, and are certainly able to maintain their home and property.

But do they want to? "Though I was still able to mow the lawn and put in the storm windows, I had done it for 40 years," said Lou, age 69. "I was ready for someone else to be responsible for the landscaping and maintenance." Lou also anticipated that he would begin to slow down over the next decade, and wanted to make the move to "carefree living" while he was still physically able to sort through his possessions.

One-level Living
The first step for many couples is to move from a larger, multi-story home to a one-level, maintenance-free townhouse, also called a patio home, condo, or connected living space. With two or three bedrooms, a living room, an eat-in kitchen, and a family room, as well as a garage and storage space, these homes are spacious enough for couples and visiting family members. And with most or all of the rooms on one floor, living is easier, even if you begin to slow down.

Like condos, these are homes that you own. Of course, if they are connected units, you may technically own everything from the interior walls inward. The condominium association usually owns the exterior walls, sidewalks, common spaces, and perhaps a pool and common room. The association will maintain these spaces, repair roofs, cut grass, and shovel snow.

To pay for landscapers and repairs, condominium associations charge a monthly fee in addition to your mortgage and taxes. Be sure to ask about this when comparing costs. You may also be required to abide by certain bylaws when it comes to the style of windows, porch light, or flower boxes on the exterior of your home.

Renting a townhome or a garden apartment could give you even more freedom. The landlord will handle the plumbing and electrical problems. You can travel without worries and still have green lawns to enjoy. Some garden apartments and high-rises are marketed specifically to seniors, so you may find many people of your own age living there.

Retirement Communities
A retirement community offers similar carefree living spaces with additional services. Many have step-down facilities, where residents relocate when they begin to need more care and assistance with the chores of daily living.

Independent Living Communities are tailored to active seniors who wish to relinquish some of the responsibilities of home ownership. You can give up some of the cooking, cleaning, and laundry by taking advantage of available services. Other amenities could include a pool, spa, wellness programs, college lectures, volunteer opportunities, entertainment, craft studios, a beauty salon, and barber services. Some communities have retail shopping, medical offices, and banking on the premises. Social activities include bus trips for theatre, shopping, or other excursions and clubs.

You may find comfort in the fact that medical, nursing, and rehabilitation services are on-site. Apartments or villas come in different sizes, with one, two, or three bedrooms, as well as studios. Many are quite luxurious and spacious. As seniors age and need some assistance, they may turn to an Assisted Living community. Here – often in the same community where you lived independently – you can receive help with bathing, dressing, and medication regimens. Rehabilitation and other medical services are also on-site.

There may also be special facilities for residents with early memory loss, Alzheimer's disease, or dementia. The staff supports these residents while allowing them to live as independently and safely as possible.

Costs are based on the size of the apartment and the services and level of care required. You may also need to pay an entrance fee to join the community. The fee may seem high, but part of this fee goes into a reserve account to pay for the assisted living or nursing home fees should you need them in the future. In some cases, your care is fully covered for however long you need it. Entrance fees vary from community to community, so check for specifics about what each fee covers. But simply put, the entrance fee pays for peace of mind.

What Is Right for You?
Susan is a marketing director for a large retirement community in the Northeast. Like many communities, this one offers independent living, assisted living, and nursing home facilities. Residents in the assisted living center receive most meals, medication, and daily living assistance. According to Susan, "They make their own decision to move in, often at the urging of their children. They prefer a simpler life; a smaller place without the worries of home ownership."

The decision to move can develop gradually. "Sometimes an accident or robbery in the neighborhood makes them realize that they are growing isolated. The kids aren't close. And they are driving less due to diminished vision or other disabilities," Susan said.

For others, a life-changing event, such as discovering a chronic medical condition or the death of a spouse or child, prompts the move. "Others are struggling with too much alone time, and want company," Susan explained. "While they may have a rational understanding that they want to move to our community, it is often hard to get used to the idea."

People often have several options to consider, much like a teenager choosing a college. There are even retirement communities that are part of a university or a golf resort. "Some people like a rural location where they can walk around the grounds; others will look for an urban setting," she said. "Consider the environment, the activities, and the culture of the place. Think about what amenities are important to you, what's not so important, and what you can live without."

When people do move to a retirement community, Susan noted, they are often impressed with the conveniences and activities. Soon they feel at home, and wonder why they waited so long.

Susan agreed that downsizing is a big process. "Some people find it liberating to give up their stuff, but for others, it's a loss," she said.

She notices that many residents bring more than they need and have boxes of dishes sitting in the garage. It often takes just a little time to break the emotional tie that connects "stuff" with a former family life. "Usually after 30 days they can't understand why they wanted it and get rid of it," said Susan. The retirement community where she works also makes use of a professional to help new residents with the downsizing and relocation process. The residents value this service and find that it's a huge benefit.

Taking It Slow

Some seniors benefit from a very gradual transition to community living. If they're not fully ready to leave their home, it can be less traumatic emotionally to spend a few days at the new apartment and a few days at their old home as they sort through their possessions.

This is what happened to Harold, the salesman we met earlier. After a stay at a medical rehabilitation facility, he needed to spend time at home in order to realize that living alone in his house was no longer a possibility.

After I helped him relocate into a new apartment, we returned to his old home once or twice a week to slowly go through his possessions. By visiting his old home and spending time with the objects that represented his former life, Harold could say a gentler goodbye and ease into his new life.

Points to Remember

- If you know an older adult who may need to downsize, slowly introduce the idea of moving to a smaller home. Some people need time to get used to the idea.

- Your home may no longer suit your needs. It may have too many stairs, require too much maintenance, and be too difficult to maneuver in.

- Consider how much you could gain by moving to an apartment or retirement community. There will be activities, a safety net, and other people to meet and befriend.

- Make the decision to downsize and move to a smaller home while you can. Illness or an injury may make the decision for you, forcing you to move when you are not ready.

- Visit apartments, retirement communities, and people who live in them to see if this kind of living might be right for you.

- If you let the idea of downsizing and moving to a smaller home sit with you for awhile, you just might like the idea.

Part Two – Don't Toss Out My Memories

"There must be more to life than having everything."
                                          -Maurice Sendak

Chapter 5: Helping Seniors Sort and Shed

Martha and Joe's decision to move brought up another problem.

After 46 years, Martha and Joe's attic is packed with the girls' old toys, school papers, clothes, and college textbooks, along with a crib, baby clothes, Christmas decorations, and old drapes. The basement is stacked with china and books that Martha inherited from her parents, who passed away several years ago.

The garage is Joe's woodworking center and houses every tool imaginable. Being there makes him think of making wonderful treasures through the years, including a baby doll cradle one Christmas long ago. In fact, precious family memorabilia was tucked under every bed and in every closet.

Cindy and Sheila know they will have to help their parents sort through their belongings before they move. "It is just too exhausting to think about it," Martha says. "How will we even get it all down from the attic?"

Fortunately, Martha and Joe realized it was time to move and made the decision on their own while they were still healthy. Thus empowered, they were able to tackle the job of gradually downsizing their possessions. This experience need not be exhausting or traumatic if handled correctly.

Start Small

After years of being the primary caretaker for her husband Fred, Anne finally made the decision to move from a very large home to an apartment in a retirement community. Though she knew this was the best choice, Anne had difficulty letting go of many of her belongings. When they were first married, she and Fred worked very hard and saved for many years to acquire a home and their many beautiful treasures.

I had been meeting with Anne for several months, helping her with the downsizing process. In her basement we came across 200 plant pots. She had once loved to garden, but had recently given it up. Yet Anne planned to move all 200 pots to her new home. She said, "I paid a lot of money for them and I am not going to waste them."

After looking over the sea of plant pots, I said, "OK. Let's go through them. Maybe there are a few that you don't really like." After looking at a few, she decided she could let go of 10 pots. Over the next month we whittled down the pile from 200 to just 10 of her favorites.

Over time, Anne realized that it just did not make sense to move all of them. This happens quite often during the downsizing process. At first, the person moving cannot bear the thought of letting go of things. But as time progresses, they "digest" the idea and realize that it is okay to let go of a few things, and then a few more. Once they grow accustomed to the idea of letting go, they are less reluctant to give up some possessions.

What's the Timeline?
Once you've decided to move to a new home, you can begin paring down your possessions. How much time will this take? It depends.

The first thing to consider is if there are any constraints or deadlines affecting the move. How much time do you have? Are you on a deadline to get out of the current house? Is a sale pending, or is a rental agreement ready to expire? Does the house need repairs before it can be put on the market?

If the home is older, in need of repair, or has a poor location, it may take a while to sell. This will matter more if you need the proceeds of the house to make payments to the retirement community or new landlord.

On the other hand, if the market is hot and the location desirable, you may find a buyer who is anxious to move in, forcing you to accelerate the schedule.

But remember that many retirement and assisted living communities have long waiting lists, so it may be months or years before a place is available. Start your research early. This will give you plenty of time to downsize your belongings while you wait for an apartment to become available.

Health is also a factor. Younger, fit seniors can sort through their possessions, lift boxes, and climb stairs more easily, and can begin long before they are ready to move. (Perhaps even just to live in a more organized way!) Older seniors will need more help and should consider hiring a professional or enlisting the help of a relative or friend. This would also be wise if you must condense the process because of an accident, illness, or sudden home sale.

And, of course, much depends on how large your house is and how many items you've collected over the years.

Thinking about these issues in advance and beginning the process early will give everyone time to adjust. You can begin to see why thinning out possessions on a regular basis and living in an organized fashion is a good idea. It helps to avoid both the physical and emotional trauma of doing it all at once.

Chapter 6: Hiring a Professional

Working with a professional organizer or senior move manager can often make the process of downsizing and moving much more manageable. A trained professional can keep things on track and lend a supportive hand without the emotional entanglement that can occur when family members or friends help seniors relocate.

Professional organizers often belong to national industry organizations. (See Appendix A for organization names and contact information.) Although certification for professional organizers is still being developed, you can obtain a high level of reliability by going through one of these organizations.

Senior move managers are similar to professional organizers, but they focus on working specifically with seniors. There are a growing number of senior move managers in the United States, and many belong to the National Association of Senior Move Managers (NASMM). (See Appendix A for contact information.)

If you are planning a move to a retirement community, check with the community's relocation coordinator for a referral to a professional. Social workers or case managers at long-term care communities, hospitals, and rehabilitation centers can also make referrals.

What to Expect from a Professional

When you interview prospective professionals, look for someone who specializes in working with seniors. Many organizers are focused on businesses, home organization, or certain age groups such as children or older adults. Be sure that the person you hire is knowledgeable about the special needs of seniors.

Here is a list of tasks that many professionals will do when helping seniors downsize. But remember that every professional is different, so be sure to ask.

Professional Services:

- Sort, pack, or dispose of possessions
- Arrange to sell or donate cars and furniture
- Meet with the movers
- Take photos of possessions
- Interact with family members
- Arrange for auctions, estate sales, and antique appraisals
- Contact museums that accept donations
- Work with real estate brokers
- Meet with retirement community management and landlords
- Suggest housing options
- Contract with cleaning services
- Arrange for computer services in new home
- Work with utility providers for connection and disconnection
- Help on moving day
- Help unpack and organize the new home
- Find kennel for pets for moving day
- Stock refrigerator
- Be a resource and make referrals for other services, such as home health agencies, home repair contractors, and geriatric care managers
- Consult on ongoing clutter maintenance after the move
- Come back after the move for more downsizing or organizing

I am often asked about services that I do not provide. In my experience, most professional organizers and senior move managers do not provide the following services. Again, remember to ask.

Services *Not* Provided:

- Give financial or legal advice
- Draft living wills, Power of Attorney, or leases
- Perform any medical care or health related nursing
- Assist with daily living tasks like bathing or dressing

If you need services that your professional does not provide, most professionals can direct you to other resources for things such as senior services agencies, meal delivery services, errand runners, and home health care workers. Your professional or a social worker may be able to recommend a geriatric case manager who can connect you with additional support resources.

A Note on the Chronically Disorganized

For some people – and not only seniors – disorganization is more than an inconvenience. Occasionally, disorganization makes it impossible for people to accomplish daily tasks, pay bills, or locate car keys. As clutter consumes the house, piles of newspapers block walkways, beds are buried under piles of clothes, and trash cans overflow.

This is more than a house that is a little bit disorganized. This is a condition known as Chronic Disorganization.

According to the National Study Group on Chronic Disorganization (NSGCD), "Chronic disorganization is having a past history of disorganization in which self-help efforts to change have failed, an undermining of current quality of life due to disorganization, and the expectation of future disorganization."

The NSGCD utilizes a "Clutter Hoarding Scale" that defines the levels of disorganization in terms of safety issues, pets and rodents, household functions, and sanitation and cleanliness. (See Appendix A for a link to information on the Clutter Hoarding Scale.) If you suspect that you or a loved one has this condition, contact the NSGCD. They can provide referrals for organizers who are trained to assist with this condition.

Organizing the Professional Way

Bertha was ready to move from her three-story home to a two-bedroom apartment. As we started working through the downsizing process, we came across boxes and boxes of birthday cards, yearbooks, photos, locks of baby hair, and other special memorabilia. Bertha wanted to keep everything, but realized that it wouldn't all fit in her new apartment.

I suggested that Bertha start weeding through it and sorting it into different categories that corresponded with different periods of her life: before marriage, travel, children, after marriage, and career. We labeled five clear containers and I guided Bertha to save only the amount of memorabilia that would fit in each container. As we made our way through the piles, Bertha was able to look at some photos, read old cards once again, and then let them go. She kept items that represented her most meaningful memories and took them to the new apartment.

Months later, Bertha's granddaughter Rose helped her make scrapbooks of all the different periods of her life. Bertha enjoyed the process of making the scrapbooks and sharing the memories with her granddaughter.

How to Work with a Professional

Understanding what working with a professional is like may help you decide if you need one to assist with the downsizing process. Keep in mind that every professional has his or her own methods, but some general things will be consistent.

During the first meeting, the professional will probably ask you about your life, including how long you have lived in your home and how attached you are to your belongings. She will also take a tour through all of your rooms, including the attic and basement.

Don't worry about cleaning up or making things look perfect before the professional arrives. There's no need to do this. After all, you engaged the professional to help you organize things and prepare for downsizing and relocating.

What you do need to have is an open and willing spirit. Be ready for a change. You must be prepared to part from things that you once loved but that are no longer of use.

If adult children are not playing an active role in the downsizing process, they can contribute best by letting the organizer help and guide their parent. It is usually best not to second-guess the parents' decisions.

As a professional, I don't work *for* my clients, I work *with* them. We'll work together in two, three, or four-hour sessions, once or twice a week, during scheduled appointments. This schedule can be accelerated if a move is imminent, but a slower process allows you to work through emotional issues between visits, mentally saying goodbye to the past and being better prepared to face the future.

As a professional, I am a guide, a cheerleader, and a motivator. "You can keep whatever you want," I say, "but let's think through this decision. Do you plan to do a lot of entertaining? Do you need china service for eight? Will the new cabinets have room for all those dishes?" I like to remind clients that they can break up sets of things, such as china. For example, consider keeping one place setting of the china that you love if you'll no longer have room for the whole set.

Long Distance Support
A professional can be a very helpful surrogate when children are geographically distant. While most professionals are usually happy to give regular progress reports to out-of-town children by phone or email, long-distance relatives also have a job to do in helping the senior downsize.

Relatives should call often and encourage the person moving to keep working on the plan to downsize. Children are helpful when they reassure parents that the professional is there to help. They can also try to keep the senior on the right track and not deter the professional from the task at hand.

An Objective Viewpoint
As a professional, I am objective, acting in an authoritative, yet compassionate, role. Because many seniors may find it easier to take advice and suggestions from someone outside of the family, the downsizing process can move along more quickly. And because I am not there to socialize, we can stick to business.

Seniors are more apt to keep appointments and do their downsizing "homework" when the directions come from a professional rather than a relative. When they know that I will be there on the same day each week, they are more likely to keep up with the necessary tasks.

In some cases, the professional may be one of the only people that a senior sees on a regular basis. For them, the professional becomes a lifeline and a companion.

Seniors sometimes share private information with me that they will not tell their children. Such information is kept confidential unless it is critical to the senior's health, finances, or a legal situation. For example, I usually find out if the senior is not eating regularly, does not sleep at night, or has become forgetful. If he or she got lost or could not find the car, they might share this with me as a funny story, but not want to "worry the children." In such cases, I would feel obligated to share this information with the children because of possible safety concerns.

Chapter 7: Decreased Possessions, Increased Emotions

Adult children and other relatives may feel some turmoil when a senior family member begins to sort through precious possessions. These emotional upheavals can cause conflicts between parents and children, between siblings, and among other relatives. But being prepared for these conflicts can help to minimize them.

As Amanda's parents reached their late 70's, their house was falling down around them. The sprawling ranch was over 100 years old and sat on three beautiful acres that Amanda's father James loved and maintained himself. Her parents had many friends in the town where they had lived for 50 years and were comfortable there. But the floor beams were rotting in the dining room, raccoons lived in the attic, and the roof needed to be replaced. The four bedrooms were in a long hallway, and Amanda's mother Peggy now walked with a cane. The long trek from one side of the house to the other was hard for her.

Peggy loved the idea of a new condo, where all the fixtures would be modern and functional. But she loved her house and enjoyed having her grandchildren visit. She knew that if they moved, their old home might be torn down, bought for the land alone. They came up with the idea of doing that now, salvaging special furnishings and building a small, one-level house for themselves. They could subdivide and sell the land to pay for the construction.

Amanda's siblings were horrified. They hated to think of the old homestead in ruins and told their parents that building a new house could be a nightmare. Somehow they thought their home would always be there to preserve their childhood memories. But the children didn't live with the termites and sagging floors.

As it turned out, re-zoning would take two years, so Peggy and James decided not to wait. They visited friends in a retirement community and were quite taken with the spacious villas, modern appliances, and many activities. They paid a deposit to secure a spot on the waiting list.

Who's the Parent? Who's the Child?

When older adults move from their long-time home to embrace a simpler lifestyle, they may also be leaving the house in which they raised their children. These children, now adults, also have emotional ties to their childhood home. Though they do not live there anymore, they enjoy visiting and going through old papers in the attic and boxes of toys in the basement. They may want a voice in the destiny of these family treasures.

On the other hand, some adult children urge their parents to downsize and relocate but are not prepared to provide the labor that is needed to do so. They sometimes forget that their parents just do not have the physical strength to take on the job.

This can be a dilemma. Grown children have their own lives, careers, and families. They are part of the group known as the sandwich generation – torn among raising their children, working, and taking care of their parents. When they can help, they may attack it in their own fashion, perhaps planning a week-long assault or a group project. This strategy can leave the older parent caught in the wake of the commotion.

When a role reversal isn't natural, parents may resent their children taking over, even if they asked for help in the first place. Frustration can build up silently and then come out over some trivial keepsake, with Mom or Dad suddenly shouting: "Stop bossing me around. This is my home and these are my things. I'll keep what I want!"

It can be equally hard for the adult children, who are sacrificing their time and possibly vacation days to help the parents move. Sometimes the adult children feel like their efforts aren't appreciated. I've heard daughters say, "Mom is acting like a child, refusing to get moving and get the job finished. I'm tempted to walk out and leave her to finish it on her own."

Seniors who are frustrated with the process may also give up on downsizing and on the whole idea of moving. I have had clients say, "Fine. Let them deal with all this when I'm gone. I don't care what happens to it." That sort of declaration sits uncomfortably with many seniors, who do care about their things and about their children. In their hearts, they know that a house full of stuff is no gift to give to a child. They know that someone has to sort through it all, but they do not know how.

Call in a Professional
This is where a professional is particularly beneficial. As an objective third-party, I do not have an emotional stake in the move. I will not miss the house when it is sold or feel bitter because my favorite tea cups were given away. Experienced professionals have some specialized skills, including a great deal of patience and the ability to really listen to their clients. As you can tell from the stories throughout this book, I often allow my clients to talk about their past and voice their

worries and frustrations. This is a key part of keeping the downsizing process on track.

Many of my clients have recently lost a spouse and are now "losing" their home and possessions, even if that last part is voluntary. They are going through several kinds of grief. And although I am not a therapist, my clients often find having someone to listen to them very helpful.

Adult children, as loving as they are, may not be ready to tackle the emotional baggage that comes with cleaning out the physical baggage. This also applies to spouses with differing points of view. Inserting a trained professional between the family members can help everyone to avoid conflict. I have heard my clients settle disputes by saying: "Well the professional said to throw it out and she knows what she's talking about." Or, "Vickie said I could keep the special things, and this is special to me."

Adult children and family members should carefully consider how much time, energy, and emotion they can devote to a senior's downsizing project. Working with a professional can help to minimize additional strain on family relationships and help to keep the peace during this upheaval.

But even with a professional in the picture, there is still plenty of room for families to argue, feel guilty, act as martyrs, and hurt one another. Below are some of the scenarios that can occur. Being ready for these situations can help you avoid them, or at least quickly recognize and resolve them.

Mothers and Daughters and Sons
Grown daughters and daughters-in-law now caring for their own families are often the first to volunteer for a downsizing

project. Daughters may feel closer to their parents than sons do, or have more flexibility in their schedules. Women are often more sentimentally attached to the family "heirlooms" and want to see them passed down to other family members.

I have seen many daughters inadvertently slip into their mother's role, deciding what goes where and what can be tossed. Invariably, Mom gets upset and says something like: "Don't tell me what to do. I've been running a household for 50 years. I'm not interested in your new ideas!" The daughter, who has taken the lead in this process and devoted many hours, is hurt and angry.

On the other hand, some mothers put their sons on a pedestal. Widows, especially, often move their sons into a "husband" role, appreciating and readily agreeing with their advice on legal and financial matters. This is even more frustrating to the dust-covered daughters, who by now are feeling like Cinderella.

Sisters and Brothers
"I'm stuck here in town, digging through all this junk, and then you waltz in with your fancy suit and claim that I'm doing it wrong."

"What gives you the right to choose your favorite Hummel figure? All you've done is throw money around."

Comments like these are all too common in the midst of a downsizing. The adult child who lives locally gets the burden of the physical labor. Perhaps another child is more financially secure and wants to spend the money on a professional. Another wants to put every trinket up for sale on eBay, while another may be bitter that he can't keep the candelabra.

The children need to sit down and have a peaceful family council to negotiate and plan a strategy. If a professional has been hired, he or she may be able to attend this meeting to help outline the work to be done and mediate squabbles.

All of the siblings should outline how they view this process, without comments or criticism from the others. One may see it as the end of Dad's independent lifestyle, while another may be delighted that she won't have to drive Mom to the hairdresser anymore. Each sibling may have different commitments and a different approach to the job of helping the parents downsize and move. If the eldest sister is able to donate a greater share of the professional fees, perhaps the younger brother can agree to devote more time to the downsizing process.

List the tasks and assign a role to each person. For example, Jack can find a good retirement community or apartment, Nancy can find a moving company and contact the utilities, and Sue can direct the downsizing while her teenage son John delivers the donations.

If adult children cannot agree to downsize according to their parent's schedule or wishes, it may be easier to let them build some distance from the situation by hiring a professional.

Consider Yourself
Children: Take some time now, even if no one is considering moving, to clean your boxes out of your parent's attic, basement, or garage. That includes your old report cards, dolls, baseball card collections, books, or wedding dress. Take responsibility for your own stuff and get in the habit of

cleaning out your own home regularly. Organization is a skill you can use for a lifetime.

Parents: Set a deadline. Anything that children or relatives are storing in your house should be removed. You should not have to sort through Uncle Max's record collection along with your own possessions. Let everyone know that anything not claimed within a certain time period will be considered unwanted and disposable.

Children: Sentiment is sticky. Give your parents permission to toss out or give away any gift that you have given them. Dad may be reluctant to throw out the ashtray you made in second grade or that orange tie you bought him during the 70s. Let them know that your feelings will not be hurt if any of your gifts end up in the trash or are given to charity.

Parents: Gifts belong to the person who receives them. That means you can return, pass along, or donate anything that anyone gave you. No one should feel guilty or insulted.

Chapter 8: What I Wish I Could Take

I started working with Ellen shortly after her son Sam convinced her that she was ready to move into a retirement community. He hired me to help her downsize her home and possessions of 38 years. For weeks, Sam, Ellen, and I worked through closets, dressers, and piles of papers, deciding what to keep.

One afternoon, Sam found a long black wig. He playfully put it on his head and asked Ellen, "How do I look, Mom?"

Ellen immediately snapped, "Take that off!" Sam started to make his way to the trash can to dispose of the hairpiece when Ellen shouted, "Don't throw that away. Put that in the save pile!"

"Mom, why do you want to save that? What would you possibly use it for?" Sam asked.

Ellen proudly replied, "I could dye it and wear it!"

Sam stomped out of the room in frustration. I put the hairpiece in our "save" pile and continued to work. Later I asked Ellen if she really planned on dying and wearing the wig. She broke down crying. "I am just so frustrated with everything that is happening in my life," she said, sobbing.

When she was calmer, we talked about all the changes that were happening in her life and how hard it was to let go of things. Since Sam became her Power of Attorney, Ellen felt like he was taking over everything in her life. He helped her find the retirement community and influenced her to move there. He was working with her doctor and paid her bills.

Ellen did not want her son to make one more decision. She wanted to be in control. And if that meant keeping that hairpiece, she was going to keep it!

Though Ellen knew that her son only wanted the best for her, it was difficult to accept the loss of control. After talking it out, she was able to let the wig go to the trash can.

What Will You Need?

When sorting through your belongings, think about where you are moving to, what services will be provided, and what other things are available there. Here are some questions to ask yourself.

- Is the new home maintenance free? If so, you can pass along that workshop of home repair tools.
- Does someone else do the landscaping? If so, you can get rid of the lawnmower and snow shovel. (If you are allowed a small flower bed, you might keep a few gardening tools.)
- Will you need two cars? Or even one?
- Is there a cleaning service? If so, take a broom and light vacuum and leave the mops and buckets behind.
- How about cooking? If meals are provided one or more times daily, you should consider cutting back on some cooking utensils. Even if you will continue with basic meal preparation, how often will you use baking pans, blenders, and fancy china?
- If you're moving to a warmer climate, thin out that closet by giving away winter coats.
- If appliances are included, your old refrigerator, oven, and freezer can be left with your house.

Will Your Furniture Fit?

Downsizing your living space usually means reducing the amount of furniture in your new home. But scaling down from many rooms to just a few is a massive job, particularly if children's old bedrooms have taken on other uses, such as a home office or sewing room.

Of primary importance is the type and amount of furniture that will fit in your new home. Get a floor plan of the new space. There are several software packages available that make this task much easier if you are comfortable with using a computer. If you are not comfortable using a software program, trace out the floor plan on graph paper. Measure the furniture and see what will fit. (See Appendix E for a furniture checklist.) Then go to the new home and measure again. The placement of windows, vents, and doors can impact what furniture will actually fit. Do not eyeball it and simply guess. Sofas often seem to gain a foot in length during the move from a big living room to a small den.

I have gone so far as to take sheets of packing paper to a new apartment and lay them out to simulate the size of the existing furniture. This clearly illustrates where passageways will be blocked and if closets doors will be restricted from opening.

A new unit may have two bedrooms and a combination living room/dining area. With fewer rooms, some spaces may have to do double duty. Perhaps a guestroom is also a sewing room, or the dining area is also a home office. Massive bookcases, tall china cabinets, and bulky sofas can crowd the available space and make it look even smaller, so think about what pieces of furniture will really be used.

Though you may have fond memories of the old couch or loveseat, two chairs might make more sense in the new, smaller living room. In the same vein, consider how the old family dining table will fit. A smaller table that seats four (with leafs to add when company comes) can work better in a new "eat-in" kitchen or dining wing. A single senior may prefer a sturdy "TV-tray" type table to eat in the living room.

This could also be the occasion to replace that 25-year old mattress with a new one. Getting a single or full-size mattress – instead of moving the double or queen – will leave more room in the bedroom for a desk or reading chair, making better use of the available space. And besides, a new mattress can be especially comfortable and help to prevent a sore back!

Finding Safe Floor Space
Rather than crowding your old living room set into a modern apartment, think about getting some new pieces that go well with the style of your new home to make the most of the available floor space.

Many seniors – now or in the near future – will need to be able to maneuver with a walker or wheelchair. That requires extra floor space between furniture and in walkways.

Remember, you can break up sets of things. You can do it with china and you can do it with furniture. Consider taking only two wing chairs and not the large sofa; or just the loveseat and only one end table; or just four of the dining room chairs. You can keep components of the things you love while still downsizing overall.

When deciding on the layout of the furniture, be sure to consider the placement of electrical outlets, heating and cooling vents, and cable, satellite, and computer hookups. Extension cords that cross walkways are a safety hazard.

This may also be the occasion to purchase a new telephone – maybe a wall unit to save space. You can also replace those older, huge consoles with a smaller stereo and a thinner, flat screen television set. Just be sure that everyone in the new home can operate the new devices.

Carefully review the lighting in the new home, and consider that older eyes work better in bright light. Some retirement villas do not have much overhead lighting, so bring your lamps and end tables or buy some floor lamps. A lamp that is adjustable and can be mounted on the wall behind a favorite reading chair is a good choice. While old lamps may still work, inspect them for loose wires that could be a safety hazard.

Chapter 9: Sorting It Out

As Peggy and James began to sort through their possessions, they took their time, enjoying rummaging through their closets and allocating items to an estate sale, charities, or relatives. "Every little bit thrown away feels like an accomplishment," said Peggy.

Their youngest son Marc spent a weekend helping out and updated his siblings on their progress: "We are continuing with our plan to work through the house room by room, drawer by drawer, closet by closet. Mom and Dad would be happy to see some things go to us."

Order Out of Chaos
Some people need to organize the accumulation of their lives before they can decide what to keep or give away. Sometimes they need to sort through their past and categorize it before they can even think about parting with it.

Items such as cards, photos, and other treasures are a vital tie to the past. To start organizing these things, sort them into piles or plastic storage boxes. Consider using a timer to limit the amount of time spent sorting and make the process feel less overwhelming. Items can be sorted by activity or time periods. This makes it easier to choose to keep just a few items from each category.

Some children might like to encourage their senior parents to tell stories about these objects. A grandchild could get involved by recording the stories on video. A videotaped collection of memories, or even a digital slide show, is much more compact than a dozen shoeboxes. I've had clients who take photos of souvenirs and create a scrapbook, quilt, or shadowbox. This is a great inter-generational project and a way for grandchildren to get to know their grandparents better.

Lightening the Load
Marc had also stored some of his own things, mostly books and memorabilia, in Peggy's and James's attic. Now he took them back to his own home and sorted through them.

A few weeks later, he sent his sister Amanda a package of letters and postcards that she had sent him over the last 15 years. His note said, "I have fondly reread many of the enclosed letters and now return them to you. Please take no offense, as I am lightening my load all around. Hold onto them if you like, read them, and let them go if you like."

Amanda picked out a few letters and postcards to make into a collage – and tossed out the rest.

Here are a few more ideas for paring down the piles.

- Remove photos from their frames and save them in an album or photo storage box.
- Scan the photos onto your computer and create a DVD to view at your leisure.
- If you can't bear to part with a 40-year old high school letter sweater or wedding gown, cut out a swatch of it and frame it with articles about the football game or the wedding invitation.
- A set of silverware or china can be broken up. Take two cups and saucers to the new house to remember it and sell the rest. You may not get as much as you would for the whole set, but in the long run, everyone will be happier.

- Wouldn't it be fun to turn an impractical crystal goblet into an elegant pencil holder?
- Toss the everyday tableware and start using the "good china" that you saved for special occasions. What are you waiting for?

When a client is indecisive about keeping an item, I like to provide some inspiration to tilt the balance toward donation or disposal by estimating the cost of moving those extra boxes of "undecided" stuff. This will usually spark some indignation: "Well, I don't want it that badly!" I also mention how much work it will be to dispose of these things later on after the move, when it is clear that the new closets will not hold it all.

From Frugal Beginnings
It is perfectly understandable to have an emotional connection to "things," particularly things from happy times in your life. But what about seemingly irrational attachments to items such as ticket stubs, plastic food containers, waxed paper, or string? Many older people hold on to such things, which is understandable when you realize that today's seniors lived through the rationing of World War II, the Great Depression, or other economic hardships. Being frugal was a way of life. It was essential to save anything that could be used again, to make good and make do. This attitude became part of their basic make-up, leading them to save stuff that may look like junk today.

This attitude is often expressed in phrases like, "That piece of fabric/glass/jar/button is perfectly good and I may need it someday." Or, "That radio/toaster/coffee pot can easily be fixed."

When my clients say these things, I always acknowledge the wisdom of frugality and even talk about how these things would have been reused in the past. Then I gently suggest that new times call for new ideas and that a bag of buttons or collection of old jars should not make the move to the new house. I suggest recycling, donating, or throwing out such items.

Here are some of the things my clients have held onto despite not using them for years.

- Used waxed paper, wrapping paper, and aluminum foil, carefully folded and saved
- Gloves, purses, girdles, and slips – formal wear from an earlier era
- Several thousand paper plates and cups
- Tablecloths and cloth napkins for formal dining
- Sheets, mattress covers, and pillows for beds that they no longer have
- Enough towels to outfit a YMCA
- Ties, belts, and suit jackets for a man who retired 20 years ago
- Enough plastic grocery bags to stock a new store
- Old wire, nails, screws, and tools

Here are some ways to loosen ties to collections of unneeded items and put them to good use.

- Review the floor plan of the new apartment and look at available storage space.
- Think about how others will benefit from items donated to a charity.

- Children's schools, camps, and day care might be able to make crafts with old buttons, paper plates, and cardboard.
- Animal shelters love old sheets and blankets.
- Vintage clothing stores and local theatre groups appreciate old dresses and suits – but only if they are in good condition. If the moths have done their usual job, throw them out.

At some point in the process, the seniors that I work with usually hit a turning point and realize that they have been overwhelmed by possessions they no longer use. "I can't believe I did this to myself. I don't ever want to be in this situation again," they say. "I've learned my lesson. It is no gift to leave this job to a child."

Hopefully, adult children who help a parent in this process will go back to their own houses and look at their own basements and attics. The easiest way to limit the job of downsizing is not to upsize in the first place. You do not have to move every five years to pare down. Just keep the memories, not the stuff.

Chapter 10: Keep, Pass, or Toss

Beatrice lived in her home for several decades. She and her husband Ted raised six children and the holidays were an especially fun time for them. From Christmas to the Fourth of July, Beatrice decorated wonderfully for every occasion.

After her husband died, Beatrice's daughters convinced her to move to a retirement community. Her daughters and I helped her through the downsizing process. They had fun going through old photos, finding surprises in boxes that were long-stored in the attic. Through tears and laughter they sorted out Beatrice's memories.

But Bea did not want to let go of any of her holiday decorations, even though they wouldn't fit into the new 800-square foot apartment. She had collected them for years and treasured them. After her house sold, she put her decorations into storage.

One day, she mentioned her collection to the administrators at the retirement community. To her surprise, they suggested that the community use Beatrice's decorations during holidays. Bea was thrilled. Not only did she get to keep and use her decorations, she could share them with others all year long.

There are various ways to sort through someone's belongings, but I find that the "Keep, Pass, and Toss" method works best. To get started, sort all items into these three categories.

- **Keep:** things that will be moved to your new home
- **Pass:** things that will be given away, sold, or donated
- **Toss:** things that need to be discarded

While Toss is a permanent decision, I often return to the Keep and Pass piles two or three times, which enables us to toss a greater percentage of items as we pare down the amount to be moved.

The **Keep** category includes everything that will make the move to the new location. It also includes items that will go into storage. This includes seasonal items, like an artificial Christmas tree, that can go in storage lockers in the new apartment complex. The only things in the Keep category are those that will be included in the move and unpacked in the new house or apartment.

If you decide to keep your beloved dining table by storing it in your daughter's garage, it only puts off the decision of eventual disposal. If a decision cannot be made, you might consider renting a storage locker until a decision can be made. Furniture should only be stored if it will be passed along to someone else within a year, perhaps to a grandchild who will soon be graduating from college or getting married and setting up a new home. Think about the ongoing cost of renting a storage locker to help yourself make a final decision sooner rather than later.

The **Pass** category includes everything that will be given away, sold, or donated. There are numerous ways that this can happen. Some involve making money from your items, while others give you a tax deduction. Still others will cost you a fee to have items hauled away.

Toss is usually the largest category. This is because Depression-Era seniors are thrifty, to the point of hoarding items that are "too good to throw away." I have seen closets full of paper bags, string, buttons, old lottery tickets, and rubber bands. Though these may have some value to an eccentric collage artist, your best bet is to consign them to the recycle bin or trash.

Passing Things On

When Harold realized he could no longer live by himself, he and I began to go through his memorabilia from his long career as a salesman. He had saved everything from his job – old pay stubs, employee handbooks, advertising campaigns, personal logs, and even a lighter with the company's logo that he received as an employee appreciation gift. His career was a very important part of his life, and he did not want to toss the evidence of his hard work in the trash. Though Harold had no close relatives, he wanted someone to remember him.

He and I visited our local historical museum and found many artifacts from churches, Girl Scout Troops, and local companies. They were interested in using some of Harold's personal records, pay stubs, and even the lighter to showcase his former employer.

Harold was pleased with the donation. He enjoys visiting the museum and is able to tell his acquaintances that he has contributed to a small piece of historical preservation.

Charitable Donations

Giving items to charity allows you to downsize and feel good about it at the same time. Many people are in need and can use a senior's unwanted household goods.

Organizations such as Goodwill, the Salvation Army, and other various groups will take furniture, clothing, and household items that are in good condition. Clubs like the Lions Club and Unite for Sight accept and recycle old eyeglasses. There are also several organizations that accept donations of medical equipment. Women's shelters appreciate donations of women's suits and dresses that are suitable for interviews and business events. Prenatal care centers may take children's clothing, baby furniture, or basic household goods. Instead of going to a landfill, organizations such as Freecycle connect people who have things to give away with others who may want them. (See Appendix B for a list of charities that may take donations.)

Libraries, museums, colleges, or local historical societies might be interested in old maps, artwork, letters, or other items of academic or historical interest. Some hospitals and nursing homes accept donations of books, magazines, and puzzles.

Old computers can be difficult, but not impossible, to donate. Some charities will take them, depending upon the age of the computer. Certain organizations will use the parts of donated computers to build new ones.. Some cities now have recycle centers for electronic items. Old cell phones can be donated to women's shelters, often through cell phone company stores. It's important to dispose of computers and other electronics correctly, since many of these items contain chemicals that can be hazardous if left in landfills. Libraries or schools might be interested in donations of DVDs or computer games if they are fairly new.

Passing along usable items to charitable organizations is a great way to help preserve the environment, help those that are less fortunate, and enjoy a bit of satisfaction knowing that items that once meant so much to you will now be used by someone else.

Resale Shops, Church Sales, and Flea Markets
Depending on the type of clothes it stocks, a resale shop may accept your old clothing. Churches and schools often accept items in good condition to resell at public fundraisers. In addition, people who have sale tables at flea markets may also be willing to take your items at no charge.

Clearing Out the Storage Area
Some organizations accept donations of used and surplus building materials. Other companies buy old doors, mantles, and windows for resale to contractors.

Many trash collectors will not take paint, chemicals, pesticides, tires, or refrigerators. Watch the newspapers or call the city sanitation department to find out about your community's next hazardous waste collection day. Or you may be lucky enough to have an organization in your area that recycles old paints and chemicals. This is the proper way to dispose of potentially hazardous substances.

Donate to the Dumpster
Although I am a big believer in recycling whenever possible, the easiest and quickest way to let go of things is to throw them away. Some municipalities have a limit on the amount of trash cans you can fill each week, in which case you may have to pay extra as you toss things out.

You might even have to call a private hauler and pay them to take the trash to the appropriate landfill. Be sure the private hauler is licensed and bonded. Your professional can help you find someone with a good reputation. 1-800-GOT-JUNK is a national franchise hauler that claims "over 338,277 customers served and 405,932 tons of junk removed." They provide dumpster rentals, labor to load the truck, and even clean up services. (See Appendix C for contact information.)

Of course, you can prevent this massive overload by cleaning out your basement, attic, and home on a regular basis.

Chapter 11: Giving to Family and Friends

After raising six children, Molly was ready to move from her large four bedroom home to a compact apartment in a new retirement community. Her husband, Dan, had passed away several years earlier and she felt ready to move on.

For decades, Molly had been the official family photographer. As we started to work together to downsize her possessions, we came across several large boxes of photos, slides, and home movies. Molly was overwhelmed. She realized that she did not have the space for everything, but could not bear the idea of throwing them away.

Her children did not want many of the items, but her daughter, Lucy, took the slides and home movies to a photo shop and had them transferred onto a DVD. Lucy made enough copies to give the DVDs as Christmas gifts to her mother and siblings that year. But the actual photographs still needed to find a new home or be tossed out.

Fortunately, Molly's annual family reunion was approaching. Inspired, she took all the unwanted photos with her and spread them out over four large tables. Cousins, nieces, and nephews were thrilled to find pictures of their families. By the end of the day, all of the unwanted pictures had found new homes. Molly was so happy that these memories did not end up in the trash, but instead brought great joy to her extended family.

Family and Friends
As you sort through your belongings, you may want to pass some things on to family and friends. But stop and think. Before passing along an item, consider the recipients' tastes.

Do they really like what you like? And are you doing your
loved ones a favor by giving them your old stuff so that it
becomes their old stuff?

It may sound callous, but just because a china teapot has been
in the family for 70 years doesn't mean it has to stay there for
another 70. Just as it is enough to keep one homemade
Valentine from when your child was small, it might be enough
to keep one of your grandmother's Hummel figures to
remember her by. What should you do with the rest of the set?
Will your children view the collection as a prized family
heirloom or just a silly set of dust-catchers? Consider selling
the rest to someone who collects the figurines and will value
them.

Think through all potential gifts. Do your children want a set
of encyclopedias, or do they do their research on the internet?
Although your niece may have often admired your hand
painted china, she may be more of a paper plate or dishwasher
type, and not really have an interest in caring for delicate
dishes. A nephew who has commented on your old-fashioned
end tables may not have any place for them in his
contemporary home.

Wouldn't your rather have your treasures displayed with
honor by a collector rather than relegated to a relative's attic?
Put the proceeds to good use to pay off some bills, help a
grandchild buy a car, or get a new, smaller sofa for the new
apartment.

While you should not use relatives as a depository for items
that you no longer have room for, some items may be perfect
for giving. For example, a grandchild or friend moving into
his or her first apartment or house might be delighted to

receive substantial, well-made furniture. And indeed, your children may be thrilled to have a piece of their childhood home. The best thing to do is ask, and never push your belongings onto others.

Avoid Emotional Chaos

Matt had been an avid hunter and gun collector most of his life. As a teenager, he collected a wide range of firearms, from rifles to historical guns from World War II. He displayed his collection in his study and enjoyed telling the history of it to anyone who was interested.

When Matt decided to move to a new apartment in a retirement community, he knew he wouldn't have room for the gun collection and tried to decide what to do with it.

His nephew Ryan loved to listen to Matt's stories about each gun. Though Matt knew the collection had some monetary value and could be sold, he felt he would rather give it to Ryan. He thought Ryan would appreciate the collection and care for it. So Matt kept a few pieces for himself and gave the rest to his nephew.

However, Matt's daughters, Nancy and Elaine, disagreed with that decision. Though they never liked their dad's gun collection, they thought it should be sold. "He could use the money to help furnish his new apartment," Nancy said. What Nancy and Elaine failed to understand was that it was Matt's collection, and its fate was totally his decision.

Matt explained to them that he did not care as much about the money as he did about the collection finding a good home with someone who appreciated it. Though they still didn't agree with his decision, they now understood why he gave the collection to Ryan.

Distribution of possessions and the sale of a family home have emotional implications for everyone in the family. Regardless of how important the move is for the health and safety of the older parents, adult children often want to keep their first home intact. Seeing pieces of their childhood, such as Christmas ornaments, books, and paintings, disappear can also be emotionally wrenching.

Add to this the inevitable disagreements about financial decisions, and the stage is set for arguments between family members that can cause hard feelings for years to come.

To avoid this type of situation, children should try to remember that the important thing is not who gets the antique hope chest. The important thing is that their parents are resettled with the belongings they need to make them happy and comfortable.

Sharing the Wealth
Naturally, you will want to do what's fair to distribute items of value or the cash you earn through a sale. But the first priority is using that income to support yourself in your new location. You will need money for the costs of the move. If you are retired and not accustomed to paying a mortgage, you may need this money to pay the rent and other fees of your new location. You may decide to sell the antiques to finance this new adventure, rather than pass them on to the family.

Many desirable items may be left once you decide what to sell and what to keep. It is up to you to decide what goes to whom, but you should ask your children and relatives, "What would you like to have from the house?"

As I already mentioned, do not be hurt if your children do not request a great many keepsakes. They have their own full houses and decorating styles. However, I often see huge arguments over who gets what.

One way to distribute prized possessions is to gather the children together and use colored dots. Each adult child gets a set of dots or stickers, one color for each person. (To keep emotional trauma to a minimum, I suggest keeping in-laws and grandchildren out of the selection process.)

The siblings walk through the house and mark any items that they want with their dot. Anything that ends up with more than one colored dot can be negotiated among the parties or given to the person who draws the longest straw.

As an alternative, you can gather collections of valuable vases, tea cups, or other bric-a-brac in one place and let children take turns picking their favorites. Again, draw straws to see who goes first. Or just let each child select one or two items and assign the rest to the antique dealer for sale.

If you have a houseful of antique furniture or valuable art or china that no one wants, sell it all through one antique dealer. Then, if you want to distribute the money to your children, divide the total sum evenly. Otherwise, your son may be annoyed that he got $300 for the Colonial style bedroom dresser while his sister got $500 for the Shaker table.

And remember, any item passed on to a child then belongs to that child. It is theirs to sell, give away, or toss out, regardless of the sentimental value to anyone else.

If you can not seem to avoid conflicts, consider bringing in a professional mediator or arbitrator. (Please, do not ask your professional organizer or senior move manager to take on this role.) Preserving family relationships is worth much more than a silver tea service.

Chapter 12: Items for Sale

As you sort through things, you may find items that have some monetary value and will not be given away or taken to the new home. Here are some options for selling certain items.

Antique Dealers
If you have truly valuable antiques or collectibles, contact a reputable antique dealer. He or she will come to your home and conduct an appraisal of your belongings. This may be needed if there is a collection of fine art, jewelry, silver, porcelain, or antique furniture involved.

There is a difference between antiques and collectibles. An antique is usually an item that is more than 100 years old, while a collectible is an item that has a high value simply because many people are interested in owning it. Toys, books, fashions, and games from the 50s, 60s, and 70s are in demand as collectibles. If you own some of these items in good condition, you may want to do a little research in your local antique malls or on eBay before giving them away.

eBay
As you probably know, eBay is a worldwide online marketplace where more than a hundred million people buy and sell goods. It is also good place to find out about the value and rarity of possessions you may want to sell.

According to eBay (www.ebay.com): "People come to eBay to buy and sell items in thousands of categories: from collectibles like trading cards, antiques, dolls, and housewares to practical items like used cars, clothing, books, CDs, and electronics."

On eBay, most items are sold through an online auction, which can be a complicated process if you are not computer savvy. However, there are also companies that will accept your items and do the legwork of selling on eBay. They will appraise your items, research their value, post and sell them on eBay, and ship them to the buyer. They return the profits to you, minus any listing fees and transaction fees. They will also take a commission fee, which is usually 30-40 percent of the selling price. What you lose in the commission fee you may make up for by using their expertise and time.

Appraisers

Appraisers will come to your house and review and appraise the value of your items. They charge a set or hourly fee. They do not sell anything for you, so they may be more objective when it comes to establishing a value for your belongings. This allows you to knowledgeably sell the items yourself. Some people also have valuable items appraised for insurance coverage.

Specialty Dealers

If you have the time and have items which are of value to collectors, you may want to contact specialty dealers. They are easy to find in the phone book or online under their specialty, such as coins, stamps, books, baseball cards, sports items, train sets, etc. Certain clothing is considered collectible, and vintage clothing shops are interested in gowns and dresses from the 1920s to the 1970s.

If you have a rare or signed first edition book, call a book dealer to come to the house and buy what they want. If your collection is more of the everyday paperback variety, donate them to a church or library for their book sale. Some nursing homes and retirement communities take paperbacks for their lending library. Used and half price book stores may also take paperbacks. Don't be surprised to get only 25 cents a book for a popular paperback. The objective here is to clear out the house, not to make money. And remember that old favorites are always available from the local library if you want to reread the books that you gave away.

Auctions and Estate Sales

Auction houses will buy your possessions wholesale, including cars and the contents of an entire house, and pay you an agreed upon amount. They then take these items to their auction house and auction them off to other buyers.

Another option is an estate sale, operated by dealers who will organize and hold the sale in your home. To make it worth their while, you need to have a good deal of quality items to sell. If they offer a "clean sweep" sale, they will put everything in the house – including old tools, old spice jars, canned goods, and jars of old nails – up for sale. Dealers will take a percentage of the proceeds as a commission.

Some senior move managers are also equipped to provide this type of service. Many have knowledge of antiques and collectibles and have the background to handle an estate sale. Just another good reason to consider hiring a professional

Take the First Offer...

Using the methods listed above can be the easiest ways to get rid of your unwanted possessions. Remember, the goal here is to downsize quickly and simply, not to make a great deal of money. Hopefully, your family had many wonderful years of using and enjoying the furniture and household goods. Do not hold onto them longer in order to get a better price.

While some items may have a great deal of sentimental value to the owner, an estate dealer values them in terms of what others will pay for them. When dealers set a market value, it is to move a particular item at a fair price, and quickly, not to make a fortune. So don't expect Great Aunt Leah's dresser to pay for the first month's rent in your new town home.

...But Don't Get Taken

Unfortunately, not all antique dealers and estate sale coordinators are reputable. Ask around and get referrals. Your professional may be able to refer you to a good dealer. Many dealers belong to professional organizations. They should be bonded and insured. Dealers should also be willing to supply references.

Though you may be tempted to hold a garage sale and keep all the profits for yourself, garage sales can be time consuming to organize, and much of the stuff often remains unsold. Placing want ads in the newspaper brings strangers into the home, and seniors can be easy targets for unscrupulous people.

Points to Remember

- Establish a timeline for the move. If possible, start early and give yourself plenty of time.

- If you do not know where to start or fear becoming overwhelmed, consider hiring a professional to assist you with the process. They can keep things running smoothly.

- Family bonds may be stretched thin during this emotional time. Be diligent about keeping the peace and enlist the help of a professional if needed.

- Think about what you will really need in your new home. Moving unnecessary items adds to the cost and time of the move.

- Make a floor plan for the furniture. Consider taking just part of a furniture set or buying new pieces that fit better in the new space.

- Donating your unneeded items to charity is a wonderful way to share your wealth.

- When giving items to family and friends, make sure the gift will be used and appreciated. When in doubt, ask!

- There are many ways to sell your items of value to help finance your move and new home. Investigate several, but don't get bogged down in trying to make a fortune.

Part Three – Moving Out and Moving In

"Have nothing in your homes that you do not know to be useful and believe to be beautiful."

-William Morris

Chapter 13: A Plan for Moving Out

Edna loved her home, especially her kitchen. She always enjoyed the chance to cook and entertain, but as she grew older she had fewer guests for dinner. Though she had managed well during her 10 years of widowhood, she knew it was time to downsize her belongings and move to a retirement community.

I started to work with Edna on the downsizing process. She had a very large kitchen filled with a substantial collection of cooking supplies. I suggested that she let go of many of these, since she was cooking less and her new kitchen was half the size of her old one. But she insisted on taking most of her cooking supplies to her new place.

When moving day came and the boxes piled up in her new kitchen, Edna finally understood the cost of her decision. After unpacking them, she made more realistic choices about what she really would use. About half of the items were packed back up and taken to a local charity, but her delay was costly. She paid to move items that she no longer needed, wasted time and energy on packing, unpacking and re-packing, and added extra stress to an already stressful moving day.

Now Edna advises her own friends not to take too much when they move to a new home. She tells them, "You can always purchase a few more glasses or plates if you really need to, but you probably won't. I don't miss anything that was sent to charity that day."

Organizing the Move
Working with a professional as you prepare to move can keep you from packing unnecessary items. Some professionals will

help you pack for your move, but others will not. Either way, let your professional concentrate on actually downsizing and organizing – it will save you money in the long run because there will be less to move!

Packing Boxes
If you and your family are packing, be sure to label the boxes. The label should state what is inside and what room the box should go in. This makes the move much smoother, and you will not need to relocate heavy boxes on your own after the movers leave.

Here are some more packing suggestions.

1. Use heavy, professional cardboard boxes for dishes and other breakables and mark them as "fragile."
2. Have a permanent marker handy for last minute notations on boxes. Also, keep a roll of packing tape on hand.
3. Have doorstops, a step stool, garbage bags, cleaning products, and bottled water available the day of the move.
4. If you cannot function without your caffeine in the morning, do not pack the coffee maker with the other appliances. Pack one box with the coffee maker or kettle, a canister of coffee or tea bags, non-dairy creamer, sugar, and filters. Have a nice wake-up cup and then transport the box in your car.
5. Pack an "Open Me First" box and mark it with brightly colored stickers or tape. This box should contain:
   - a small lamp and light bulbs, in case it gets dark before you finish unpacking;
   - a knife, box cutter, or scissors for opening boxes;
   - toilet paper and a box of tissues;

- a few paper cups, plastic utensils, and paper plates for that first meal;
- granola bars or other non-perishable snacks;
- pillows, sheets, and blankets for the bed;
- towels and soap;
- the pet's food dish, a serving of food, and bedding;
- a telephone; and
- paper towels and a spray bottle of all-purpose cleaner in case you need to wipe down the bathroom or kitchen shelves before putting things away.

Also pack a suitcase with a change of clothes, pajamas, toiletries, cosmetics, and medication. This will make it easier to find these essentials without rummaging through boxes before bedtime. Keep things like cash, wallets, checkbooks, and cell phones in a separate bag and put it somewhere easy to locate and hard to lose.

You can ask for free used boxes at the office supply shop or local liquor store. You can also buy sturdy boxes from a moving company. I recommend that you buy at least a few "professional" boxes for more delicate items. Moving companies also supply wardrobe boxes that allow you to transport a closet full of clothes on their hangers. These boxes are collapsible so you can keep them for a future move. Or leave them standing to store out-of-season clothing.

Hiring Movers Versus Do-it-Yourself
If you don't want to pack your own boxes, let a moving company do it! Movers are very experienced in this area and can save you time and frustration. In particular, you can minimize breakage of fragile items such as kitchen dishes or figurines by allowing movers to pack those items.

Renting a truck and moving heavy furniture may have worked when you were in college or your first apartment, but a 50-year old back is not as flexible as a 20-year old one. If you are thinking of doing it yourself, get lots of help from young, strong neighbors or relatives.

Hiring a moving firm will save your muscles and your patience. Professional movers have the process down to a science, and they can empty a house, load a truck, and unload it far faster than you or I. They can also carry very heavy items down winding staircases and take dressers filled with clothes, eliminating lots of packing and unpacking. Generally, the skilled pros will also move your possessions with fewer nicks, scrapes, and twisted ankles than the family will be able to do.

Interviewing and Hiring a Moving Company
If you are working with a professional, he or she may be able to arrange for and contract with a moving company for your relocation. Organizers and senior move managers have far more experience working with movers than most individuals. Plus, they can recommend good companies who have exhibited professionalism and courtesy.

If you are downsizing and coordinating the move yourself, here are some tips on hiring a moving company. Ask around for recommendations from someone who was happy with their moving experience, perhaps a neighbor in your new community. Look for a firm that has been in business for a long time and ask for experienced employees.

Often, the initial phone call with a moving company can reveal the level of service that you can expect. When you talk with potential movers, ask the following questions. If possible, get the answers in writing. And always read the contract before you sign it.

1. How many workers will help during the move?
2. What time will they arrive and how long will the whole move take?
3. What guarantees do I have?
4. How will I be compensated if the movers are late or do not show up?
5. What happens if the truck breaks down?
6. Who should I call if there is a problem on the day of the move?
7. Will I lose a deposit if I have to cancel?
8. How much am I insured against breakage? Do I get the value of the item when I first bought it, as a used item, or the replacement value?
9. Do the movers know how to get to _____ (the new home)?
10. Will they get directions or should I provide them?
11. Will they pack the boxes on the day of the move or the day before?
12. Is packing included in the estimate? Is it an hourly rate or am I paying only for materials?
13. Is anything not included in the estimate?
14. Will the movers bring packing materials, padding, tape, markers, and labels?
15. Do I need to empty the dresser drawers?
16. Will the movers bring blankets for the furniture and pads for the elevator (if required)?
17. Is there anything they will not move, such as plants or valuable antiques?

If possible, be sure to tell the moving company coordinator what the crew can expect on the other end, such as elevators, limited parking, narrow halls, or winding staircases.

When deciding what to take with you, consider if there will be extra charges or added difficulty in moving large items such as a refrigerator, piano, or dining room set. Also, find out ahead of time if these items will fit in the elevator and through doorways at the new home.

What to Expect from Movers

Most moving firms will send a representative or a move coordinator to your home ahead of time. They will walk through the premises and review the furniture, appliances, and belongings that will be involved in the move.

If you have not finished downsizing by this time, be sure to tell the coordinator what furniture, appliances, or boxes are not part of the move, so they are not included in the estimate.

On moving day, make it very apparent what is going and what is not. I have seen movers pack and move garbage cans with trash in them, along with tools that belonged to the neighbor! Be sure to have everything clean and cleared out on moving day.

The moving personnel should be on time and bring the previously agreed to number of people. They should be planning to stay as long as arranged or as long as it takes. They should have all the equipment, the proper vehicles, and packing materials. If any of these factors do not match the original arrangements, call the moving company immediately; they may be able to rectify the situation on the spot. On the other hand, if your plans change, notify the movers in advance.

Do not feel the need to be overly accommodating if the moving company alters their plan. If the company sends two people instead of three, or a smaller truck instead of the required size, they will just have to make extra trips and spend extra hours until the job is done.

On the other hand, remember that moving is very hard work. It's a nice idea to treat the movers to lunch or tip them for their effort. You may also want to pack some protein rich snacks, cold drinks, and ice in a cooler. The movers will certainly appreciate it.

What the Movers Shouldn't Move
Make sure that the items being handled by the movers are insured. Check with the moving company about the level of insurance needed. There is always a chance that something will happen, and some items may be lost or damaged. Because of this, there are some things that you should consider moving yourself. This is similar to taking a carry-on bag with you on a plane. While some possessions can be replaced with insurance money, things like family photos could be gone forever.

Here are some items that you should move yourself.

- Personal papers, stock certificates, insurance documents, and health records
- Cash and checkbooks
- Address books and lists of phone numbers
- Plants
- Jewelry or other valuables
- Refrigerated or frozen food in a cooler

- Pets
- Irreplaceable paintings in glass frames and other delicate, breakable items
- Prescription medications
- Irreplaceable, sentimental items such as scrapbooks, diaries, photos, and home movies

If you have a pet, consider treating it to a little vacation on moving day. By staying with a friend, family member, or even the local kennel, pets can avoid the trauma of moving day, stay out of the way, and not become a runaway when open doors and misdirected attention abound.

Utilities and Your New Address
Remember to cancel the utilities at your old house, but don't do it too soon. Better to pay for an extra day than not to have phone service on moving day! Also, ask the landlord or move coordinator at your new community what utilities they provide. If you need to arrange things yourself, find out who to contact for the phone, cable, gas, and heat. They may need to be turned on and put in your name.

Update your address for newspaper and magazine delivery as well as credit card bills, and be sure to forward the mail. Your professional may be able to do some of this for you, but some companies require that the individual who holds the account, or their appointed Power of Attorney, handle these things. (See Appendix D for a handy moving checklist.)

Chapter 14: A Plan for Moving In

After living in their one-story home for decades, Lucas and Thelma were ready to move. It had become difficult for them to manage when Lucas began using a walker and Thelma needed a cane. When they decided to move to the assisted living section of a retirement community, their out-of-town sons, Pat and Steve, hired me to help them with the downsizing and relocation process. Everything went smoothly and moving day was soon upon us.

When we got to the new apartment, Lucas and Thelma wanted to help unpack and supervise the move. Although the one-bedroom, one-bath apartment was small, it was just the right size for them. I suggested that they relax in the lobby while the movers unloaded everything into the apartment. They were hesitant at first, but as the movers came in with loads of boxes and furniture, they quickly understood why. Their apartment was soon crowded with three movers, me, and my assistant. I was also afraid that Lucas and Thelma would get hurt in all the commotion and was glad when they agreed to get a cup of coffee in the lobby.

After the movers finished, my assistant and I emptied a few boxes and got some furniture in place (based on the room design we'd previously established). Lucas and Thelma then returned to do the fine tuning.

As I unpacked the kitchen dishes, Thelma gave suggestions as to where they should go. Lucas had definite ideas about how his office supplies should be arranged. In this way they helped with the organizing without doing the actual unpacking. In short order we had the furniture placed and some boxes unpacked. Empty cartons were moved outside and we soon had room to maneuver.

Lucas and Thelma now understood that making themselves scarce was the best thing they could do, even at that crucial time. They were also very happy that they did not have to supervise the furniture placement and unpack all those boxes!

In addition to helping you get ready to move, professionals can be very helpful on the other side of the move, when it comes to unpacking. We can unpack and organize closets and cabinets in the new location, and make it easier for you to cope in this smaller space. Check with your professional to see if he or she offers this service.

Coordinate with Your New Home

Retirement communities and apartment buildings usually have move coordinators and maintenance people on staff to help with your move. They can assist with many details and may have specific requirements for you to follow.

Contact them early in the process to reserve the day that you want to move in. Be sure that your apartment will be vacant and clean. Will you be able to get in? Do you have a pass and parking permit for the community gate and a key for the apartment?

Remember to work with the coordinator of the community when planning your move. The coordinator will need to know the date and time of your arrival. She will also make sure that there is room for the moving truck to park near the entrance. You may also need to reserve the elevator for a set time and number of hours. This is why your moving team needs to arrive on time and pack quickly.

To protect their interiors, most elevators need to be padded before any furniture is moved onto them. Ask if the community has pads for the elevator, and measure the height of the elevator (or the stairwells.) This will help you determine if that extra long headboard will fit.

Ask about any special requirements. I have worked with communities that only allow their own maintenance staff to hang paintings, install computer or phone lines, or alter the electrical set up (like installing a dimmer switch). You will want to schedule this for the day of, or shortly after, the move.

Use the Floor Plan
If you have followed my suggestions and created a floor plan for the furniture, be sure to have it handy when the truck is being unloaded. If the couch is carried to the right spot the first time, it will not have to be moved again. This makes the movers happy, which is one of your chief objectives. Happy movers are more careful with your belongings. Don't forget: Movers who do a good job deserve a tip, and doing so is customary.

Before you pack, take photos of the knickknacks on the dresser, mantle, or dining room hutch at the old house, so you can duplicate the look in the new home. This can help you feel at home more quickly. Also duplicate the arrangements of the kitchen and bathroom as much as possible so you spend less time searching for a can opener or hair brush.

The First Night
Sometimes, you may not be able to sleep in your new home the night of moving day, depending upon the size of the move and how comfortable you need to be that first night. The

power may not have been switched on or the bolts to reassemble the bed may be on the floor of a moving van. Keep your suitcase with a change of clothing, pajamas, and essential toiletries on hand and arrange for an alternate place to sleep the night of the move.

After a long, stressful day of moving out and saying farewell to your old home, having a nice dinner and a good night's sleep will help enormously. Consider staying in a hotel or with a friend that night. Some communities have a furnished unit on the premises that can be rented by the night, which is also a great idea.

If you do not have the help of family, friends, or a professional, do not try to do a lot of unpacking that first evening. In the morning you will be rested and ready to unpack and organize your new home.

If you're helping a senior who might become disoriented in a new place, consider staying with them for a night. Put a nightlight in the hallway and bathroom to help light the way in an unfamiliar setting. Be sure that all hallways are clear of boxes and clutter. And find out how to contact security or other staff and share this information with the senior. It's essential to know who to call if the senior feels dizzy or accidentally locks you – or themselves – out.

Chapter 15: Saying Goodbye and Settling In

Harriet and Tom lived in their two-story home at the end of a quiet street on the edge of the woods. The location was a great place for their four daughters to play ball in a field of trees. They had moved in when their oldest daughter, Carla, was two years old. Each year they marked the occasion by etching the date and her height on the casing of the basement door. As the years passed, every daughters' height was measured and etched into the door frame, marking memories of little girls growing taller.

When Harriet and Tom decided to give up the house after 43 years and move to an apartment, they downsized their belongings and furniture. They thought about the wonderful new life they would have at the retirement community and looked forward to the transition.

On moving day, the movers arrived promptly and proceeded to pack the truck. At one point, Harriet remembered something she needed out of the basement. As she started to open the door, she glimpsed the row of lines on the door frame and burst into tears. "Oh my," she thought, "Are we doing the right thing? What if we don't like it there? Our life is here. This is our home; we can't sell it to someone else!"

Harriet cried for awhile and so did Tom, but they knew their decision was the right one. I reassured them that it was normal to be sad about leaving a place you love. We took a picture of the etchings in the door frame to preserve their memory. The move proceeded and all went well.

I visited Harriet and Tom a month later to see how they were settling into their new apartment and was glad to learn that they loved it. They had even hung the picture of the door frame etchings by the front door of their new apartment.

Leaving their home was hard, but they knew it was the best decision they could make. The new family that now lives in the old home is equally delighted with the field of trees, giving Harriet and Tom a special satisfaction.

When preparing for a move, remember that this is the first step of a great journey and a fresh start. You will be able to let go of the problems of home ownership. Although you are letting go of things and places, you will never lose the memories.

Consider having a small ceremony or gathering to say goodbye to your old home. Invite some family and friends over to share their memories and videotape their recollections of being in your house. Take photos of the little things: the rug inside the front door, the squeaky step, or the torn screen on the back door. Dig up a few flowers from the yard and put them in pots to take to the new house.

However, do not hold this ceremony during the chaos of moving day. Take the time throughout the downsizing process to say goodbye to your home in a meaningful way. Let everyone take an item to help them remember the family house. Ask them to write down and bring along a special memory. Perhaps someone will volunteer to edit it, add some photographs, and create a special scrapbook as a keepsake of your old home.

Unpacking the Right Way
I usually try to unpack most of a client's boxes and make the apartment livable in a day or two. But I am more than willing to let clients think about the arrangement of the smaller

details. And while you should not expect to do it all in one day, do not let it drag on for weeks. You want to be able to live your new life, enjoy your new home, and have it ready for visitors.

If you want help, ask your family and friends to join you for a day of unpacking. But feel free to tell volunteers that you are in charge and that you decide where things should go.

However, as an organizer, I feel obliged to encourage systems for easier living and point the way to an organized lifestyle. If a client wants to put coffee cups on the second shelf and a cake platter on the first shelf, I gently point out that items she uses more often should be the most accessible. But in the end, everyone must respect the seniors' wishes. After all, it is *their* new home.

Finding Storage in Unexpected Places
Though downsizing before the move was important, creating organization and eliminating clutter in your new space is equally important. Here are some tips to expand your new home to give you space for the things that are important to you.

- If the walk-in closet is roomy, put a dresser in the middle or against the back wall.
- Use back-of-the-door hanging organizers for shoes, belts, hats, and gloves.
- If physically capable of using one, get a secure, easy-to-handle step stool so you can store and retrieve lightweight items from the tops of shelves.
- Consider buying specialty hangers that conserve space by securing more than one skirt or pair of pants on a hanger.

- Put hooks on the backs of doors for bathrobes. Consider a hook near the back door for a sweater or coat.
- Use shelf helpers and mug hooks for coffee mugs in kitchen cabinets.
- Use small organizing baskets in pantries to keep like food items together.

One of my clients no longer took showers, only baths, so she converted her extra shower into a storage space for cleaning products and laundry detergent. Don't be afraid to get creative – just keep it organized.

Staying organized will make your life more convenient. Store like items together. Put food in one cabinet, dishes and glasses in another. Put all the cleaning supplies in one closet and the medicine, cosmetics, and soaps in the bathroom. Office supplies should stay together in a desk drawer for easy bill paying and letter writing.

Using Vertical and Hidden Spaces

Even after going through your possessions, you may still have things which you use just a few times a year, such as holiday decorations, a special cake platter, or a Hanukah menorah. When space is tight, consider storing these things way up high or way down low.

If you are buying new furniture, consider pieces that have built-in storage. There are hope chests that can be used as coffee tables, ottomans with drawers, even beds with built-in storage space. Many end tables and TV stands have room for movies, books, or magazines.

You can also purchase narrow cabinets that fit into small spaces. Small shelving or drawers, often on wheels, fit between the toilet and the sink and are great for storing bathroom supplies. A shelving unit can also be set on top of the toilet tank to create shelf space there. Kitchen and bath stores have many useful pieces that can quickly expand your storage options without shrinking your wallet.

When closet space is at a premium, under-the-bed storage boxes can be used to keep out-of-season clothing flat and neat. Another option is to fill suitcases with out–of-season clothing and store them under the bed. This keeps both suitcases and the clothing out of sight, but easy to get to. Extra sheets and towels, perhaps for guests, can also fit in suitcases.

Vertical space also includes the top shelves of the closet, the tops of kitchen cupboards, and the top of the coat closet. Just be careful or ask for help when you need to get something down. Many seniors have fallen off step ladders or unsteady chairs and been saddled with a broken wrist or ankle as a result.

Before purchasing any type of organizing product, be sure that you really need it and that it makes sense for your needs. Also measure the space where you plan to use the product before buying it to make sure it fits.

Staying Safe
If you or a loved one has relocated to a retirement village to be safer, do not sabotage the effort by creating an unsafe apartment. Many older adults have trouble walking, so thick rugs can be dangerous obstacles, particularly for those using canes or walkers. I call throw rugs "tripping mechanisms."

Make sure to secure all carpets and rugs with carpet tape or rug pads.

Too much furniture and too narrow walkways can cause stubbed toes, trips, falls, breaks, and bruises. Make sure the furniture layout leaves ample room for walkers and wheelchairs. (And get those moving boxes unpacked and out of there!)

Make sure everyone knows how to get out of the apartment in an emergency, particularly if it is a high-rise, and ask the staff to run through the fire drill procedure. Here are some additional precautions.

- Be sure rooms are well lit, so you can see where you are going. Older eyes need more light to see well.
- Don't string electrical cords across the room. This can obstruct walking and create a fire hazard.
- Be sure there are grab bars in the shower, the bath, on all stairs, and perhaps near the bed. Decals on the bathtub floor help to prevent slipping.
- There may be a pull chain in the bathroom that serves as an emergency cord to alert a nurse or attendant. The retirement community staff will show you how to use it.
- Make sure that curtains, dishtowels, and pot holders are hung well away from the stove. As age increases, memory may decrease, and burners can be left on by accident. Another way to prevent fires is to limit the use of candles.
- For security, be sure that you can close all the doors and windows easily and know how to lock and unlock them.

Chapter 16: After the Move

Abigail and her husband Frank were married for 48 years when Frank died. They had enjoyed a wonderful life and raised four daughters and one son.

A year after Frank's death, Abigail gathered up all her memorabilia. She found cards and love letters from Frank, Mother's Day cards from her children, holiday cards, her grammar school report cards, and many other mementos. She also found her wedding dress and veil.

Frank and Abigail owned a cabin in the mountains where they spent many long weekends and most of their summers for several decades. One autumn weekend, Abigail decided to go back to the cabin. She packed up her memorabilia, including the wedding dress, and headed out to the cabin for a long autumn weekend of sorting through it all.

She enjoyed her time reminiscing, sitting in front of the large stone fireplace. As she read through the piles of cards, letters, and mementos, she laughed a lot, cried a little, and tossed each one into the fireplace. She even burned her wedding dress.

This made perfect sense to Abigail. After Frank's death, she started to think about the end of her own life. She just did not like the idea of her children reading through her personal items after her death and then throwing them away. "If anyone was going to discard these precious memories, it was me," she told me. "So I laughed, cried, and burned my mementos. This was the right thing to do and the cabin was the perfect place to let it all go."

Avoid Accumulations

Once you have downsized and relocated, take some steps to make sure you are never overwhelmed by possessions again. Stuff is less likely to accumulate in an organized home, and a "don't keep it" mentality will also go a long way.

Six months after their move, I often revisit my clients for another downsizing. By this time they are often ready to get rid of things that landed on the "keep" side of the decision the last time around. Boxes of holiday cards and bereavement cards have been reviewed and are ready for tossing. The reality of living in an overcrowded apartment is sinking in and a few more trinkets make their way to charity.

They will soon realize how nice it is to be organized and how easy it is to find things in a well-organized home. If they want life to stay this easy, they must avoid accumulation. Here are some changes that will help you stick to a more organized way of living.

- Cut down on junk mail by asking companies not to send mail and catalogs. The Mail Preference Service (MPS) assists consumers in decreasing the national non-profit or commercial mail they receive at home. (See Appendix C for more information.)
- Sort your mail immediately. Keep a trash can handy and throw out unwanted mail as soon as it comes in. Don't let things pile up to read "someday." If you don't get through the March *Readers Digest* by the time April's issue arrives, put the old issue in the recycle bin or donate it to your local library.
- Better yet, consider sharing newspapers and magazines with other in your new community, perhaps by leaving them in a common area for everyone to read. This

saves money, eliminates trash, keeps apartments tidy, and encourages friendships. You can also develop a shared collection of games, books, and jigsaw puzzles. Start thinking of these things as communal items and free up your closets.

- Older adults often encourage more mail by responding to sweepstakes and contests. Telephone solicitations might also result in additional mailings. It is okay to hang up on unwanted solicitors. This may also eliminate sales from telemarketers who prey on the kindness of older adults and sell them unwanted and unneeded items.
- To cut down on telemarketers, join the National Do Not Call Registry. According to the Do Not Call website, the Federal government created the national registry to make it easier and more efficient for you to stop getting telemarketing calls you don't want. Registration is free. (See Appendix C to get on the National Do Not Call Registry.)
- Some seniors ask their adult children to handle their finances and bills. To keep important bills and paperwork organized, make one, well-marked accordion folder to keep everything together. Then a trusted relative or friend can come by once a month to review the papers and pay the bills.
- Keep things like stock certificates and important legal documents safe in a bank safety deposit box.

Gifts for the Storage-challenged
Just as you do not accept dessert when you are on a diet, do not add more stuff to your slimmed-down and resettled lifestyle.

While many of us love to shop and receive gifts, I suggest that those with limited storage space let go of something every time they gain a new possession. In comes the new toaster, out goes the old one. Stick with your clutter-free, organized lifestyle.

However, this policy makes gift giving – and receiving – a little tricky. Encourage loved ones to buy you non-tangible gifts like luxury services or things that you can use up. Here are some clutter-free gift ideas to share with your family and try out yourself.

- Buy gift cards for a restaurant, coffee house, spa or beauty parlor, afternoon tea, taxi ride, errand or cleaning service, car wash, or oil change.
- Pay for an hour or two of a professional organizer's time to help with that second thinning out.
- Give tickets to the theatre, a sporting event, a lecture, or enough tickets to take a few friends to the movies.
- Pay the registration fees for a class at a senior center or community college.
- Stamps, soap, and stationery are appreciated and used up regularly.
- Give tickets for a trip or tour. While a cruise is wonderful, even a bus or boat trip around your own city can be fun.
- Diabetic approved candies or other hard-to-find special diet items are a nice treat.
- Create a certificate good for five "free" car rides so the person using it never has to feel like they are imposing when they need a lift.
- Pay for cleaning or cooking services.
- Baskets of fun, non-perishable food are nice. A collection of treats such as snacks, a bottle of wine, or

specialty teas and coffee can feel like an indulgence, especially to someone on a limited budget.
- Make a charitable contribution in a loved one's name. Local service organizations, public radio and television stations, libraries, museums, and hospitals are always looking for donations.

Emotional Rollercoaster Ahead

People who move to a retirement community, especially those who previously lived alone, may find it to be very different from their past lifestyle. They may be unhappy at first as they get used to their new environment. They may spend less time alone. Depending on the level of care they are receiving, activity coordinators, neighbors, nurses, cleaning staff, and maintenance people will drop in throughout the day. Many senior citizen communities make a point of visiting their residents, just to see how they are doing.

Eating with other people may also be a big change. The food may be different from what they normally eat, and may come in larger or smaller portions. Having set hours for meals can also be an adjustment. All this just takes some getting used to, and options are usually available, so ask.

If you're the one living alone, try not to take all of your meals in your room or apartment. And if your loved one is isolating herself, suggest that the dining room is a good place to get acquainted with others. Seniors usually eat healthier food if they do not have to prepare their own meals.

Even the noises are different in a new home. To someone who lived in a house, sharing a hall with other people's chatter, televisions, and radios – not to mention cooking smells and pets – can be a difficult adjustment.

The religious and spiritual activities of the new community may be more or less than you expected. This is something you should check out ahead of time, to be sure that your spiritual leanings are compatible with the philosophy of the community leadership.

If your parents express complaints to you, you may feel like all of your efforts to make them happier have been in vain. Keep in mind that change is hard, and remember the advantages that have been gained. While seniors who relocate may lose some privacy and independence, they gain convenience, safety, more of a social life, and security.

If you've moved to a new location and are having trouble adjusting, try taking advantage of the activities your new community offers. This can help you see the positive side of your new lifestyle. Consider joining a committee, offering to teach a class, supervising a gardening group, or volunteering to plan a party. It's easier to get used to your new environment when you're engaged and enjoying yourself.

Points to Remember

- When hiring a moving company, ask questions about how the workers operate and what to expect from them during the move.

- Move irreplaceable items yourself, including cash, checkbooks, jewelry, special photos, and any other extremely valuable items.

- Have someone watch your pet on moving day, so Fido does not get in the way or get lost.

- Get help to unpack so you do not become overwhelmed.

- Utilize vertical and hidden spaces in your new home and use organizing products to help keep you organized.

- Orient yourself to your new surroundings.

- Instead of receiving material gifts, request gifts that do not require storage space, such as gift certificates or edible items.

- Give yourself time to adjust to your new home.

- Getting involved in activities is a great way to begin enjoying this new phase of life.

Part Four – The Seniors of the Future

"An open home, an open heart, here grows a bountiful harvest."

-Judy Hand

Erin arrived back home after spending three exhausting weeks helping her parents pack up their possessions and move to a retirement community. She had tried for several years to encourage her parents, Ralph and Mary, to downsize and move, but they could not bear the thought of leaving their home of 54 years. Finally, health issues forced them to move.

Erin knew the downsizing and relocation process would be a daunting task, but she had no idea how physically and emotionally exhausting it would turn out to be. She spent 10 days going through the attic, basement, bedrooms, and kitchen, "arguing" with her parents about what to keep and what to let go. She finally ordered a dumpster and filled it to the brim.

Now the house was sold and the closing was at hand. Not only had Erin run out of time to complete a more thoughtful downsizing process, she was emotionally unable to face another day of old boxes. Though her parents were upset at seeing their memories tossed unceremoniously in the trash, they understood that Erin didn't have a choice. She had to take over and plow through their home or it would not have gotten done. Her parents finally understood why they should have cleared out those rooms periodically over the years.

After Erin's parents settled into their new home, she considered the experience and started to look around her own house. Though her sons are now teenagers, she still has their action figures up in the attic, "just in case they want them someday." Erin decided, "Someday is now."

Everything came down from the attic, things were tossed, given away, and some things went back up for storage. After her experience with her parents' home, she had a different view about "holding on to stuff that you might want someday."

Erin was not going to leave her sons with the task of downsizing her belongings as she aged. She wanted to make her own decisions and resolved to downsize once a year, just before her birthday. The downsizing weekend has become a ceremony, one that she sometimes shares with friends, as she clears out closets and drawers, honoring and commemorating each stage of her life.

The seniors of the future – those who are 30, 40, or 50 years old today – will be a different sort of older adult when they downsize their homes at age 60, 70, 80, and beyond. Many different factors are contributing to a cultural shift that will drastically alter the "golden years" after 2025. Though, perhaps by then, we will be calling them our "platinum years."

For one thing, the seniors of the future may not live in one house for 30 or more years. They move more often than their parents would have dreamed of doing. Sometimes couples are looking for a new location or just want a more modern home. Adults who follow their career paths around the world will relocate for a better job, and couples may even keep two homes to maintain a bicoastal lifestyle. Sometimes a hobby that requires a specific location – like the ocean for deep sea fishing or clear, dark skies for astronomy – prompts people to move.

If you move frequently, it gives you the chance to clean out and throw things away more often. Trim down your possessions to make each move a little easier. Some of these future seniors will live unburdened, not dragged down by buying and owning lots of things. Of course, others will not.

Not All in the Family

The rapid pace of the world today has made adults more accustomed to change. They do not hold onto a telephone for 20 years because technological advances may make it obsolete in just two. Old televisions, tape recorders, and even computers grow useless quickly and should be recycled immediately, instead of being stored in the attic, garage, or basement.

Tomorrow's seniors are also less likely to hold on to the past emotionally or be ultra-frugal since they didn't live through the Great Depression of the 1930s as their grandparents did.

Today, family connections are more fragile, and traditions less respected. Many younger adults would rather sell a valuable family possession and spend the money where they need it or would more enjoy it. They easily decide to sell a set of fine china they do not use in order to buy something that they will use.

The rise of eBay sales has made this even easier. I have seen families sell boats and antique cars that are too expensive to maintain. Antique tablecloths that must be ironed, china that must be hand washed, and pianos that need regular tuning are all regarded as too much trouble to keep, and too valuable not to sell. Art and jewelry that require insurance also go on the digital auction block.

From Life to Lifestyle

Many of today's active young professionals are not house-proud. When they are not working and relaxing, they want to spend their time skiing, traveling, and pursuing hobbies. In order to spend time playing, they hire people to mow the lawn, clean the house, and maintain the swimming pool.

As these young adults age, they may turn their backs on house-husbandry altogether, and move to a low-maintenance condo or retirement community in their late 60s or 70s. These younger, healthier seniors may choose condominium living to make their lives easier, avoiding yard work and housework. They may choose this lifestyle so they can travel more often, without the responsibilities of home ownership.

People who move more often and concentrate less on their homemaking must keep their possessions under control. Without organization, a carefree, mobile lifestyle is impossible.

Tips for Staying Organized
Even if you aren't planning a move in the next few years, you can downsize for a more organized lifestyle today.

Sort through your belongings now, using the downsizing techniques described in previous chapters. Pretend you are moving. You do not have to give away or pass along things that you love, but you can designate them for specific people or charities. A label in an inconspicuous place can make your desires known. You can also invite your children to select their "inheritance" now. Join them as they go through the family treasures and select a favorite.

Use new technologies to digitally save photos, movies, and music. Use a digital scanner to save paper memorabilia such as play programs, wedding invitations, and hand-made greeting cards without taking up physical space.

Do not accept other relatives' "treasures" if they will simply sit in your attic. Give your own children a deadline to get their books, toys, and school reports out of your basement. College graduation is a good time to do this. Having the boxes clutter up their first apartment will be a real incentive to slim down their own possessions.

Where have you stored important papers, collections, vintage clothing, and photo albums? Are they safe from water damage, mold, moisture, insects, and animals? If you value something, don't let it be ruined by neglect.

As a gift to the next generation, take some time on a rainy day to identify the people in your family photos. If you have more photos than you want, label them and send them off to the subject's family or descendents.

Keep It All Under Control
Though it may be many years before you are ready to downsize your possessions and move into a smaller home, there are some good reasons to begin the process now.

First of all, you will make it much easier on your children and loved ones when the time comes to clear out your home. And let's face it, the future is uncertain and changes can arrive unexpectedly. No matter when the time comes, you'll be giving them a wonderful gift by staying organized.

Secondly, you will enjoy the benefits of living in a scaled-down, well-ordered home. Just think: once you have pared down your possessions to what you really need and love, you will be living in a sea of organization.

And third, never again will you have to search through overstuffed closets to find a pair of gloves or hunt through a desk to find a lost bill or checkbook. You can make dinner more efficiently without a clutter of unused pots and pans in the cupboard.

Of course, organized living goes beyond keeping less stuff around, but downsizing your belongings is a good first step. You can use the techniques described in this book to get started. A professional organizer can teach you additional ways to live as an organized person.

Having more things than we know what to do with may be a sign of a wealthy society and a prosperous family. And yet, there are so many people in our world that do not even have the bare necessities. Looked at it from that point of view, downsizing and distributing your belongings, and limiting yourself to what you really need and love, can truly be a shared blessing.

Appendices
Finding Professionals

The National Association of Professional Organizers (NAPO)
www.napo.net
Formed in 1985 as a not-for-profit professional association, NAPO is dedicated to sharing information about the organizing industry and defining quality standards for the organizing profession. To find a professional organizer near you, visit the website.

Professional Organizers in Canada (POC)
www.organizersincanada.com
The POC was conceived in 1999 and now has over 300 members. Professional Organizers that belong to this organization can be found on their website.

The National Association of Senior Move Managers (NASMM) www.nasmm.com
NASMM is a non-profit, professional association of senior move managers dedicated to helping older adults and their families with the physical and emotional aspects of moving. It is committed to maximizing the dignity and autonomy of older adults as they transition from one living environment to another. The website can help you locate a Senior Move Manager in your state.

The National Study Group on Chronic Disorganization (NSGCD)
www.nsgcd.org
The National Study Group on Chronic Disorganization is a non-profit group. Its mission is to explore, develop, and disseminate information to professional organizers and related professionals about organizing methods, techniques, approaches, and solutions that will benefit chronically disorganized people.

Clutter Hoarding Scale:
For information regarding the NSGCD Clutter Hoarding Scale, please visit **www.nsgcd.org/gp/factsheets_gp.html**.

Charities

For household, furniture, and clothing donations:

- Goodwill Industries International, Inc.
  www.goodwill.org

- The Salvation Army
  www.salvationarmy.org

- Society of St. Vincent de Paul, Inc.
  www.svdpusa.org

For eyeglasses:

- Lions Clubs International
  www.lionsclubs.org

- Unite For Sight
  www.uniteforsight.org

For medical supplies:

- Global Links
  www.globallinks.org

This is just a small sampling of national charities that take donations. Please check your local listings for additional organizations. Also check with the charity in your area to see if anything has changed regarding their donation acceptance policy.

Useful Information

- Find out how to remove your name from a mailing list at **www.dmaconsumers.org/offmailinglist**.

- To add your phone number to the National Do Not Call Registry, call 1-888-382-1222 or visit **www.donotcall.gov**.

- Instead of sending unwanted items to a landfill, Freecycle is non profit organization that connects people who have things to give away with others who may want them. For more information, visit **www.freecycle.org**

- Earth 911 provides earth-friendly ways to dispose of many items that can be difficult to dispose of and some that may be hazardous to the earth. Visit **www.Earth911.org** or 1-800-CLEANUP.

- Find a hauler to take away your old stuff by calling 1-800-GOT-JUNK or visiting **www.1800gotjunk.com**.

Moving Checklist

Current Address:

Name:_____

Address:_____

City: _____ State: _____ Zip: _____

Phone: _____ Email: _____

Moving to:

Name:_____

Address:_____

City: _____ State: _____ Zip: _____

Phone: _____ Email: _____

Approximate moving date: _____

Packing Day

Date: _____ Starting Time: _____

Moving Day

Date: _____ Starting Time: _____

This person will supervise the packing and moving at the old

home: _____

This person will supervise the moving and unpacking at the

new home: _____

Move coordinator at new community:

Name:_____

Address:_____

City: _____ State: _____ Zip: _____

Phone: _____ Email: _____

Notification given to new building of move in: _____
                                                      Date/Time

Who did you talk to? _____

Elevator at apartment building reserved for the move at this

time: _____

Other requirements they may have for the move:

_____

_____

_____

Downsizing Process

☐ Downsize belongings and make decisions about what to bring.

☐ Make decisions on furniture.

☐ Schedule weekly 3-4 hour sessions with organizer to make decisions about items.

Room	Date Completed
Living Room	_____
Dining Room	_____
Kitchen	_____
Office	_____
Basement	_____
Family Room	_____
Attic	_____
Garage	_____
Master Bedroom	_____
Bedroom #2	_____
Bedroom #3	_____
Bedroom #4	_____
Bathroom #1	_____
Bathroom #2	_____
Bathroom #3	_____
Other	_____

☐ Make list of furniture that will be going.

☐ Design furniture floor plan for new home.

☐ Take unwanted better quality clothes to clothing consignment store.

☐ Take unwanted used clothes to charity.

☐ Allocate one room to collect items for estate sale (if needed).

Auction

Name:_____

Address:_____

City: _____ State: _____ Zip: _____

Phone: _____ Email: _____

Estate Sale

Name:_____

Address:_____

City: _____ State: _____ Zip: _____

Phone: _____ Email: _____

Charitable Donations

Name:_____

Address:_____

City: _____ State: _____ Zip: _____

Phone: _____ Email: _____

Date and time of pick up: _____

Movers Being Considered

Name:_____

Address:_____

City: _____ State: _____ Zip: _____

Phone: _____ Email: _____

Estimate: _____

Name:_____

Address:_____

City: _____ State: _____ Zip: _____

Phone: _____ Email: _____

Estimate: _____

Name:_____

Address:_____

City: _____ State: _____ Zip: _____

Phone: _____ Email: _____

Estimate: _____

Selected Mover

Name:_____

Address:_____

City: _____ State: _____ Zip: _____

Phone: _____ Email: _____

Meet with move coordinator on _____ (date)

Deposit of $_____ paid on _____ (date)

Who will give directions to the moving company to get to new home?

Name:_____

Address:_____

City: _____ State: _____ Zip: _____

Phone: _____ Email: _____

Who will meet the movers at the new home?

Name:_____

Address:_____

City: _____ State: _____ Zip: _____

Phone: _____ Email: _____

Utilities
Transfer, discontinue, and reconnect utilities.

Electric
Company:_____

Address:_____

City: _____ State: _____ Zip: _____

Phone: _____ Email: _____

Account Number: _____

Date of disconnect from old home: _____

Date of connecting/transfer to new home: _____

Gas
Company:_____

Address:_____

City: _____ State: _____ Zip: _____

Phone: _____ Email: _____

Account Number: _____

Date of disconnect from old home: _____

Date of connecting/transfer to new home: _____

Water
Company:_____

Address:_____

City: _____ State: _____ Zip: _____

Phone: _____ Email: _____

Account Number: _____

Date of disconnect from old home: _____

Date of connecting/transfer to new home: _____

Sewage
Company:_____

Address:_____

City: _____ State: _____ Zip: _____

Phone: _____ Email: _____

Account Number: _____

Date of disconnect from old home: _____

Date of connecting/transfer to new home: _____

Trash

Company:_____

Address:_____

City: _____ State: _____ Zip: _____

Phone: _____ Email: _____

Account Number: _____

Date of last service at old home: _____

Date of first service at new home: _____

Landline Phone

Company:_____

Address:_____

City: _____ State: _____ Zip: _____

Phone: _____ Email: _____

Account Number: _____

Date of disconnect from old home: _____

Date of connecting/transfer to new home: _____

Cell Phone (if moving out of local area)

Company:_____

Address:_____

City: _____ State: _____ Zip: _____

Phone: _____ Email: _____

Account Number: _____

Date of disconnect of old phone: _____

Date of connecting/transfer to new phone: _____

Internet

Company:_____

Address:_____

City: _____ State: _____ Zip: _____

Phone: _____ Email: _____

Account Number: _____

Date of disconnect from old home: _____

Date of connecting/transfer to new home: _____

Cable/Satellite Dish

Company:_____

Address:_____

City: _____ State: _____ Zip: _____

Phone: _____ Email: _____

Account Number: _____

Date of disconnect from old home: _____

Date of connecting/transfer to new home: _____

Landscaper/Lawn Service

Company:_____

Address:_____

City: _____ State: _____ Zip: _____

Phone: _____ Email: _____

Account Number: _____

Date of last service at old home: _____

Date of new service at new home: _____

Cleaning Service
Company:_____

Address:_____

City: _____ State: _____ Zip: _____

Phone: _____ Email: _____

Account Number: _____

Date of last service at old home: _____

Date of new service at new home: _____

Newspapers
Paper Name:_____

Address:_____

City: _____ State: _____ Zip: _____

Phone: _____ Email: _____

Account Number: _____

Date of last delivery at old home: _____

Date of first delivery at new home: _____

Paper Name:_____

Address:_____

City: _____ State: _____ Zip: _____

Phone: _____ Email: _____

Account Number: _____

Date of last delivery at old home: _____

Date of first delivery at new home: _____

Magazines

Magazine Name:_____

Address:_____

City: _____ State: _____ Zip: _____

Phone: _____ Email: _____

Account Number: _____

Date of last delivery at old home: _____

Date of first delivery at new home: _____

Magazine Name:_____
Address:_____

City: _____ State: _____ Zip: _____

Phone: _____ Email: _____

Account Number: _____

Date of last delivery at old home: _____

Date of first delivery at new home: _____

Magazine Name:_____
Address:_____

City: _____ State: _____ Zip: _____

Phone: _____ Email: _____

Account Number: _____

Date of last delivery at old home: _____

Date of first delivery at new home: _____

Mail Forwarding
Old Address:_____

City: _____ State: _____ Zip: _____

Phone: _____ Email: _____

New Address:_____

City: _____ State: _____ Zip: _____

Phone: _____ Email: _____

Change of Address form sent in to U.S. Post Office (or done online): _____

Date Forwarding Will Start: _____

Banks
Bank Name:_____

Address:_____

City: _____ State: _____ Zip: _____

Phone: _____ Email: _____

Account Number: _____

Bank Name:_____

Address:_____

City: _____ State: _____ Zip: _____

Phone: _____ Email: _____

Account Number: _____

Retirement Accounts

Name:_____

Address:_____

City: _____ State: _____ Zip: _____

Phone: _____ Email: _____

Account Number: _____

Name:_____

Address:_____

City: _____ State: _____ Zip: _____

Phone: _____ Email: _____

Account Number: _____

Social Security and Pensions

Name:_____

Address:_____

City: _____ State: _____ Zip: _____

Phone: _____ Email: _____

Account Number: _____

Name:_____

Address:_____

City: _____ State: _____ Zip: _____

Phone: _____ Email: _____

Account Number: _____

Insurance

Homeowners Insurance Company:_____

Address:_____

City: _____ State: _____ Zip: _____

Phone: _____ Email: _____

Policy Number: _____

   ☐ Notified of date of move

Life Insurance Company:_____

Address:_____

City: _____ State: _____ Zip: _____

Phone: _____ Email: _____

Policy Number: _____

Medical Insurance Company:_____

Address:_____

City: _____ State: _____ Zip: _____

Phone: _____ Email: _____

Policy Number: _____

Medicare:_____

Address:_____

City: _____ State: _____ Zip: _____

Phone: _____ Email: _____

Policy Number: _____

Doctors and Dentists

Doctor Name:_____

Address:_____

City: _____ State: _____ Zip: _____

Phone: _____ Email: _____

Doctor Name:_____

Address:_____

City: _____ State: _____ Zip: _____

Phone: _____ Email: _____

Doctor Name:_____

Address:_____

City: _____ State: _____ Zip: _____

Phone: _____ Email: _____

Dentist Name:_____

Address:_____

City: _____ State: _____ Zip: _____

Phone: _____ Email: _____

Pharmacy Name:_____

Address:_____

City: _____ State: _____ Zip: _____

Phone: _____ Email: _____

Home Health Care Service Name:_____

Address:_____

City: _____ State: _____ Zip: _____

Phone: _____ Email: _____

Social Worker:_____

Address:_____

City: _____ State: _____ Zip: _____

Phone: _____ Email: _____

Health Care Professional:_____

Address:_____

City: _____ State: _____ Zip: _____

Phone: _____ Email: _____

Others
Real Estate Agent:_____

Address:_____

City: _____ State: _____ Zip: _____

Phone: _____ Email: _____

Handyman:_____

Address:_____

City: _____ State: _____ Zip: _____

Phone: _____ Email: _____

Notes:

Furniture Checklist

Current Address:

Name:_____

Address:_____

City: _____ State: _____ Zip: _____

Phone: _____ Email: _____

Moving to:

Name of Community: _____

Move-in Coordinator: _____

Address: _____

City: _____ State: _____ Zip: _____

Phone: _____ Email: _____

Wish List of furniture that you would like to take with you:

_____

_____

_____

_____

Kitchen

- ☐ Kitchen Table _____ (Dimensions)
- ☐ 4 chairs _____ (Dimensions)
- ☐ Coffee Maker, Toaster Oven, Blender, Food Processor
- ☐ Dishes and Silverware (set for 4, 6, or 8)
- ☐ Pots and Pans
- ☐ Bakeware
- ☐ Utensils
- ☐ Radio, Hand Vacuum, TV
- ☐ Microwave _____ (Dimensions)

Other kitchen items:

_____

_____

_____

Living Room

- ☐ Couches _____ (Dimensions)
- ☐ Coffee Table _____ (Dimensions)
- ☐ Chairs _____ (Dimensions)
- ☐ Flower arrangements/Plants/Centerpieces

☐ End tables

☐ Table Lamps ＿＿＿＿＿ (How many ?)

☐ Standing Lamps

☐ Wall Lamps

☐ Paintings

☐ China Cabinet ＿＿＿＿＿ (Dimensions)

☐ TV and TV stand ＿＿＿＿＿ (Dimensions)

☐ Stereo ＿＿＿＿＿ (Dimensions)

Other Living Room items:

＿＿＿＿＿＿＿＿＿＿＿＿＿＿＿＿＿＿＿＿

＿＿＿＿＿＿＿＿＿＿＿＿＿＿＿＿＿＿＿＿

＿＿＿＿＿＿＿＿＿＿＿＿＿＿＿＿＿＿＿＿

Dining Room

☐ Table ＿＿＿＿＿ (Dimensions)

☐ Chairs ＿＿＿＿＿ (Dimensions

☐ China Cabinet ＿＿＿＿＿ (Dimensions)

☐ Buffet ＿＿＿＿＿ (Dimensions)

Other Dining Room items:

_____

_____

_____

Den/Office

☐ Couches   _____ (Dimensions)

☐ Small Table   _____ (Dimensions)

☐ Chairs   _____ (Dimensions)

☐ End table   _____ (Dimensions)

☐ Table Lamps   _____ (How many?)

☐ Standing Lamp/ Wall Lamp

☐ Paintings

☐ Book Shelves   _____ (Dimensions)

☐ Desks   _____ (Dimensions)

☐ Filing Cabinets   _____ (Dimensions)

☐ TV and TV stand   _____ (Dimensions)

☐ Stereo   _____ (Dimensions)

Other Den/Office items:

_____

_____

_____

Hallway

☐ Side Tables   _____ (Dimensions)

☐ Paintings   _____ (Dimensions)

☐ Chair   _____ (Dimensions)

Other Hallway items:

_____

_____

_____

Bathrooms

☐ Shower Curtain

☐ Bath Mat

☐ Waste Basket

☐ Hamper

Bedroom (1)

- ☐ Bed with headboard   _____ (Dimensions)
- ☐ Nightstands with lamps _____ (Dimensions)
- ☐ Dresser   _____ (Dimensions)
- ☐ Mirror
- ☐ Small Dresser   _____ (Dimensions)
- ☐ Hope Chest   _____ (Dimensions)
- ☐ TV and TV stand   _____ (Dimensions)
- ☐ Stereo   _____ (Dimensions)
- ☐ Chair   _____ (Dimensions)
- ☐ Chest of Drawers   _____ (Dimensions)
- ☐ Waste basket

Bedroom (2)

- ☐ Bed with headboard   _____ (Dimensions)
- ☐ Nightstands with lamps _____ (Dimensions)
- ☐ Dresser   _____ (Dimensions)
- ☐ TV and TV stand   _____ (Dimensions)
- ☐ Stereo   _____ (Dimensions)
- ☐ Chair   _____ (Dimensions)
- ☐ Mirror
- ☐ Waste basket

Other Bedroom items:

_____

_____

_____

Notes

About the Author

Vickie Dellaquila is a Certified Professional Organizer® and senior move manager, and president of Organization Rules, Inc., based in Pittsburgh, Pennsylvania. Through her business she has helped many clients de-clutter, organize, and simplify their lives.

She uses her background in nursing and social services to help seniors downsize and relocate. Her expertise enables her to answer questions like: "I have lived in a five-bedroom, two-story home for the past 47 years and need to downsize and move. How do I start?"

Vickie is a member of the National Association of Professional Organizers (NAPO) and a founding member of NAPO Pittsburgh. She is a current board member and marketing director for NAPO Pittsburgh, and a member of both the National Association of Senior Move Managers (NASMM) and the National Study Group on Chronic Disorganization (NSGCD).

Her company has been featured in several local publications, including *Pittsburgh Post-Gazette*, *Pittsburgh Tribune Review*, and *The Pittsburgh Magazine*. She also writes a regular column for HOME Design and Remodeling Resource Guide magazine.

For more information please visit:
www.OrganizationRules.com

Vickie lives in Pittsburgh with her husband, three daughters, and miniature schnauzer in an uncluttered, simplified house.

Senior Move Management Services

Do any of these situations apply to you or someone you know?

You are relocating to a retirement community and have a house or apartment packed with many years' worth of memories, and you do not know how to start sorting through it all.

You want to help your parents move from their large home to a smaller one, but you live out of state. Or maybe you live nearby, but your life is just too busy to allow you to be of much help. Do you need someone to help you help them?

Organization Rules can help. We provide downsizing and relocation services for seniors who are moving to a smaller home or retirement community. We take the stress and worry out of the downsizing and relocation process for seniors and their families.

For more information please contact us at 412-913-0554 or vickie@OrganizationRules.com.

Learn more online at www.OrganizationRules.com.

Professional Organizing Services

Organization Rules provides professional organizing services for those who are overwhelmed and frustrated with the disorganization in their life and home. In many cases, your belongings can take over your home. People are tired of managing it all. You want to be organized, but you just can't seem to do it by yourself.

Organizing is a process and by becoming organized it can lead you to a simpler, less stressful lifestyle. Having less things to manage is easier. Getting organized will not only transform your home and life, but it also may change how you feel about your belongings.

Organization Rules can help you through the frustration and with feelings of being overwhelmed by helping you get organized with a plan and tools you will need. We provide residential organizing services that help you let go of items no longer wanted, free up time to do the things you really want to do, and help you think differently about bringing more unwanted things into in your home. We provide guidance, support, and the help for you to succeed. If you are ready and would like some help, we are here to help you transform your home and life.

For more information please contact us at 412-913-0554 or vickie@OrganizationRules.com.

Learn more online at www.OrganizationRules.com.

Organization Rules Business Guide

Have you thought about starting your own senior move management business? Do you enjoy de-cluttering and organizing? Do you have the patience and passion to help seniors through some very stressful events in their lives? Are you not quite sure how to find more information, or how to get started in this business?

Organization Rules, Inc., provides personalized services to individuals looking to start their own senior move management business. Put the experiences and knowledge of Vickie Dellaquila, Certified Professional Organizer®, to work for you.

For more information, please visit:
www.OrganizationRules.com
or call 412-913-0554

Move Management Workbooks

Do you like the moving and furniture checklists in the back of this book? Now you can order copies of these checklists to use on your move! Using large print, these workbooks are intended to be written in. There are even pages to sketch out a floor plan for your new living space!

To order workbooks, visit:
www.OrganizationRules.com
or call 412-913-0554

To order additional copies of this book, please visit

www.OrganizationRules.com